SKYLINE

Cultural Memory
in
the
Present

Mieke Bal and Hent de Vries, Editors

SKYLINE

The
Narcissistic
City

Hubert Damisch

Translated by John Goodman

STANFORD UNIVERSITY PRESS

STANFORD, CALIFORNIA 2001

Stanford University Press
Stanford, California

© 2001 by the Board of Trustees of the
Leland Stanford Junior University

Printed in the United States of America
on acid-free, archival-quality paper

Assistance for the translation has been provided by the
French Ministry of Culture

Skyline: The Narcissistic City was originally published in
French in 1996 under the title *Skyline: La ville Narcisse*,
© Éditions du Seuil, April 1996.

Library of Congress Cataloging-in-Publication Data
   Damisch, Hubert.
   [Skyline. English]
   Skyline : the narcissistic city / Hubert Damisch ;
translated by John Goodman.
      p.   cm. — (Cultural memory in the present)
   Includes bibliographical references.
   ISBN 0-8047-3245-0 (alk. paper) — ISBN 0-8047-3246-9
(paper : alk. paper)
   1. Symbolism in architecture.   2. Architecture—Classification.
3. Symbolism in architecture—United States.   I. Title.   II. Series.
   NA2500 .D3413   2001
   720'.1—dc21   00-064088

Original Printing 2001
Last figure below indicates year of this printing:
10   09   08   07   06   05   04   03   02   01

Typeset by James P. Brommer in 11.5/13 Garamond

Contents

Preface

Skyline, n.: the line where earth and sky meet; the horizon.

What follows is not so much an attempt at an inventory as it is a set of exercises that I would call "topographical," for they deal with places, to some degree imaginary and symbolic, that Western thought has used, or in which it has become invested, at various historical moments and in various ways, in the process of constituting itself, of finding its bearings (the bearings of the "subject," itself Western, even its "American" variety). The city; the labyrinth; the museum (insofar as it encompasses architecture); but also America (whose discovery coincided with a decisive moment in the history of the said subject); the island of Manhattan; the great open spaces of the American West, natural parks, and other sites ostensibly retaining something of their first wildness: places that lend themselves to functioning as *scenes,* of everything from history to dreams, and as scenes of writing such as can be read on the walls of the city, from highway interchanges to movie screens, the movies having posed anew the question of representation's relation to that which ostensibly provides its site or scene, literally as well as figuratively.

"Topographical" aptly characterizes these exercises insofar as they bear on realms that are identifiably spatial, however imaginary they might be. But the designation is apt, too, because these texts aim to tease out some of the rhetorical uses and speculative investments that these "places" have favored and continue to favor, to say nothing of the effects they tend to foster in the logical or symbolic order. Thus we will see how, from Descartes to Freud, the relation of thought to its habitat has been radically transformed in ways related to the discovery, after that of America, of the unconscious. But while the archaeology of the city—and preeminently of Rome, the city often designated "eternal" in the West—provided Freud with a model for visualizing the layered structure of the unconscious, and the establishment of the "natural" parks and reserves so characteristic of American culture provided him with an apt metaphor for illuminating—in the sense we say that notes or glosses are designed to illuminate the meaning of texts deemed obscure—the role assigned to *fantasy* in the psychic economy, a problem arises immediately regarding the link between these rhetorical conceits and the two Freudian "topographies": apart from a few theoretical asides that are far from systematic, the following exercises—they are indeed "exercises" and not "essays," a distinction to which I shall return—adopt an essentially descriptive approach to what might be called subject sites and thought habitats. In the end, the problem will be to effect a transition from an inventory of places that is in principle selective (implicit in the very idea of an "exercise") to something that constitutes a *topique* in the narrow sense, which is to say a *theory*.

Having thus established the horizon against which these exercises stand out, and toward which they strive to advance, we can extend the metaphor, and even reverse it: Freud's use of visual images to illuminate his own "topographies"—the first one distinguishing the three registers of consciousness, preconsciousness, and the unconscious; the second one breaking the unconscious down into the id, the ego, and the superego—affords insight into the selection, redistribution, and imbrication of sites established by thought, not to mention the subject, when it (whatever its gender) projects itself onto them. These images or metaphors are the result of an operation analogous to that of which space itself, as an *a priori* category of perception in the Kantian sense, is the product. Such, at any rate, was Freud's belief, if we are to credit one of his manuscript notes: "Space might be a projective extension of the psychic apparatus. Probably no other derivation. Instead of the *a priori* conditions of the psychic apparatus according to Kant. Psyche is extended; knows nothing of this."[1]

Space—not to mention time—being here less an a priori category of perception than the correlative of an operation whereby sensation itself—and, through its mediation, the "psyche"—accesses the exterior world by projecting itself onto it: the exercises that follow set out to track, especially on the level of rhetoric, some of the adventitious effects of the unconscious determination known as *projection*, without pretending either to grasp it fully or to pursue all of its temporal ramifications, which entails certain problems, theoretical as much as rhetorical.

One of the century's greatest prehistorians, J. Gunnar Andersson, when the time came for him to assess his work, described the difficulties inherent in his project: whereas scarcely a century ago almost nothing was known of China's prehistory, within a period of some fifteen years (from World War I to the 1930s) archaeologists managed to assemble a collection of data that, while fragmentary, was sufficient to cast some light on the period prior to the earliest legendary dynasties. The author found himself faced with two options: he could pretend to "fill out synthetically the voids in our knowledge" by proposing reconstructions; or he could relate only what he had himself observed, allowing the reader to fill in the unwritten pages "according to his taste." But not without providing this reader—as Freud had done in a completely different context, with every bit as much archaeological rigor as the Swedish historian—with all the information he deemed pertinent regarding the circumstances and even the history of these discoveries; beginning with that, in which he himself had taken part, of the first remains of the now celebrated *Sinanthropus Pekiniensis*, or "Peking Man." As if these circumstances, as if this history were integral, in the strongest possible sense, to a discovery that by its very nature was bound to deck itself out in the seductive trappings of narrative insofar as this can be reconciled with gaps and the fragmentary. (As Nietzsche said, through his mouthpiece Zarathustra: "And when my eyes flee from the now to the past, they always find the same: fragments and limbs and dreadful accidents—but no human beings!"; poetry—and psychoanalysis itself, a close relative of history in this regard, and especially of prehistory, when it is not governed

by a totalizing impulse—striving to consider and reassemble into
"One"—a construction that, at the very least, has meaning despite
or even because of these gaps, just as one is obliged to work with the
gaps when assembling a puzzle—that which is "fragment and riddle and dreadful accident."[2])

Likewise remarkable is the fact that the archaeologist went so
far as to compare the spatial arrangement of archaeological data to
the projection of a movie in a dark room:

Layer after layer of fossil-bearing strata follow each other in endless numbers, just like the pictures in a film. Just as the film lies rolled up and life-
less until it is set in motion and until the beams of an electric arc-lamp
project it, so also the fossil remains lie silent and unintelligible in their
rock beds until scientific research illumines them with its penetrating
searchlight.

And the analogy, Andersson continues, can be taken farther:

Then scene after scene followed, a mass of supernumeraries: tribolites,
brachiopods, mussels and corals. . . . But it is only when we reach the first
mammals in the Eocene deposits of the Yellow River and in Shantung that
the intensity of the performance is increased and we are completely captured when the white screen reveals the splendid pictures from the *Hip-
parion* steppes. . . . And finally there appears on the scene the Douglas
Fairbanks of the prehistoric drama, the Peking man.[3]

For my part, I offer no narrative accounts of any discovery.
And I leave it to the reader, should such be to his taste, to interweave
some of the strands that I have intentionally left disparate here, or to
supply some missing pieces of the puzzle (how Tokyo, even more
than Beijing, as Denis Roche pointed out to me, is henceforth un-
usable for topographical or speculative purposes; the present-day
theatrical scene; and so forth). However, the movie metaphor strikes
me as quite apt (allowing for the fact that my stars of reference are a
couple, Fred Astaire and Cyd Charisse, whereas when J. Gunnar Andersson was writing his book Peking man still lacked a partner) insofar as the essence of film is understood to be strictly narrative,
whereas the space within which it operates or that it establishes be-

comes visible only via the double detour effected by projection and by the movement that this imprints on images that are themselves still (unlike the mode of projection used in painting and geometry, but not unlike that operative in the translation of dream thoughts into images).

Setting aside the fact that several of them resulted from occasional commissions, if the texts that follow are better described as "exercises" than as "essays," that is because, with one or two exceptions, their "author," or he who occupies this site, is neither openly implicated nor directly at issue in them, which does not preclude his having inscribed himself within them by projection, or imply that the incessant displacements by which the reader is invited to pass from philosophy to architecture, from antiquity to the modern era, from Europe to America, from Herodotus to Tocqueville, from Descartes to Freud, to say nothing of references, explicit in these instances, to times when I frequented movie theaters, encountered America, its incomparable cities and spaces, and traveled to Berlin, that all of these exercises don't posit, outside the bounds of the present collection, something like a narrative. A "story," if you like, but one that accrues meaning only if curled up inside that ecological niche where thought has too long believed it could find shelter; inside that dubious object (like the *tableau* in painting) which, at a time when computers can so easily manipulate and store text, has lost all fantasmatic resonance, although perhaps not all formal advantages; in that other place, just as improbable as the ones that will occupy us here, but whose exigencies and resources, despite everything, one way or another, whatever the contraints, we must work to preserve and maintain: the book.

Among other things, this particular book will turn on the image of the city and the desires—too often disappointed—that it nourishes. In *Mauvaises Pensées et Autres,* Valéry introduces a vestigial dialogue between a statement placed within quotation marks, like a citation, and a comment on it by the author, who carefully underlines a word corresponding to one of the crossroads of his thought:

"C'était une Ville de rêve . . . "
Il ne s'agit donc pas d'*architecture.*[4]

"It was a City of dreams . . . "
Thus there is no question of *architecture.*

But how are we to understand this? And, first of all, how are we to understand the proposition within quotation marks: "C'était une Ville de rêve . . . "? Is the City in question—its first letter capitalized—something about which we can dream, or is it a concept conducive to dreams? Are we to understand that this City is one that exists only in dreams? A kind of "ideal" City, to the extent that the ideal is reconcilable with dreams? A City of dreams, or a nightmare City, like Borges's City of the Immortals, which—if dreams indeed satisfy desires—would imply that, if dream (or nightmare) there be, it would have things to tell us about City desires, about desire in the City, about the City as object of desire. About the City of which we dream, or could dream, without worrying about whether or not this dream could become reality.

The assertion that there is no question here of *architecture*—I again stress Valéry's underlining of the word—is all too likely to trouble anyone who, in the matter of cities, is interested primarily in their form or aspect; in the form and aspect of the City; in the City as form or aspect, and that form (or aspect), as we shall see, eminently narcissistic. Is this to say that architecture has nothing to do with dreams, any more than it has to do with desire, not to mention its relation to the city? Or—not necessarily the same thing—that the desire, the need for architecture is not one that can find satisfaction in dreams? Given that dreams, at least "City dreams," are by no means architectural, subject to the laws and constraints of architecture? But what is it, then, that determines the difference between dreams and architecture—a difference so irreducible that it seems to be a contradiction in terms to speak of "dream architecture."

In Valéry, the word *architecture* has a precise, essentially constructive resonance. In his dialogue "Eupalinos," when Phaedrus and Socrates evoke, from the land of the dead, the immense effort expended on the construction of so many celebrated cities and use-less monuments, a process in which reason nonetheless plays its part (otherwise, Phaedrus agrees with Socrates, everything "would be leveled"), it is in the course of a discussion of *construction*, Phaedrus having begun by reminding Socrates about the building they had witnessed, when alive, in Piraeus. And when Phaedrus describes his encounter with Eupalinos, the architect of the temple of Artemis, whose beauty Socrates has extolled to him, it is to observe how, af-ter having seen it rise, he cannot separate the idea of a temple from that of its construction. Not being much of a dreamer, Eupalinos conceived much as he executed: "What I think, is feasible; and what I do, is related to the intelligible."[5] Or, as Phaedrus puts it: "Destroy-ing and constructing are equal in importance, and we must have souls for the one and for the other; but constructing is the dearer to my mind."[6] And how could it be otherwise, given that *construction* per se is preeminently a mental affair? "What are buildable things? Those, exclusively, that involve mental operations."[7] Its being un-derstood, of course, that—unlike those philosophers whose great misfortune it is, according to Valéry's Socrates, never to see the col-lapse of the universes imagined by them—any worthwhile thought will yield to and accord with the principles of solidity, utility, and beauty governing architecture. This observation also applies to what is known today as "deconstruction," seeing as the latter bears on sys-tems of thought and on the ideological effects produced by this very architecture: it is well for Valéry to present Socrates the constructor as the anti-Socrates; Plato's Socrates already practiced a form of di-alectic able to put all discursive constructions to the test, even to dis-mantle them.

The City poses a question, then, as does landscape on other grounds, insofar as both are conducive to dreaming, whereas archi-tecture scarcely stimulates this, and indeed tends to thwart it. And we should remember the analogy noted by Valéry between architec-ture and the book: not in order to reinvigorate archaic fantasies of the Book or antiquated bibliophile cults but rather, where Valéry rightly reproached architectural typography[8] (as I will try to do here with public graphics), with the intention of retaining the constraints imposed by the form "Book," the demands that it makes, the proofs that it requires: the said form assuming its full meaning when a book brings together materials many of which had previously been scattered; in the vain hope that, however aleatory it might be, when it doesn't adhere to a design at odds with architectural reality, the resulting construction might be of some use, that it might withstand criticism and, through the grace of reading, be illuminated by a few rays of light.

SKYLINE

PART ONE

THE
NARCISSISTIC
CITY

1

Street Window

November 1619. Sequestered in his "stove-heated room" on the banks of the Danube, where he had been delayed by the first cold of winter en route to rejoin the army of the duke of Bavaria, Descartes tried to put his thoughts in order. And, among them, one that would serve as preamble to the articulation of the principal rules of method in his *Discourse on the Method*, where, upon being stated, it is cast as a metaphor that I will retain here by way of frontispiece: the well-known image with which the philosopher tries to persuade his reader that the best way to lead one's life is to strive to think for oneself, using only one's own reason, without bothering about received ideas or the opinions of others, this image effectively appeals—beyond the walls of the room where Descartes conceived the first idea for the *Discourse*, even beyond the limits of the "quarters" to which he was then restricted—to the register of architecture and, without further transition, to the idea, to the measurements and forms, to the external appearance, if not the internal disposition, of the city, understood historically, and even in its generative principle:

Thus we see that buildings undertaken and completed by a single architect are usually more attractive and better planned than those that several have tried to patch up by adapting old walls built for different purposes. Again, ancient cities which have gradually grown from mere villages into large towns are usually ill-proportioned, compared with those orderly towns [*places*] that planners [*un ingénieur*] lay out as they fancy on level ground. Looking at the buildings, you will often find as much art in them, if not more, than in those of the latter; but in view of their arrangement—a tall one here, a small one there—and the way they make streets crooked and irregular, you would say it is chance, rather than the will of men using reason, that placed them so. And when you consider that there have always been certain officials whose job it is to see that private buildings embellish public places [*servir à l'ornement du public*], you will understand how difficult it is to make something perfect by working only on what others have produced.[1]

Insofar as the reader can conjure for himself a visual or aural idea of what the text says, the site serving as a framework for the *Meditations* by this same Descartes—a well-heated chamber—differs from that in which he had previously conceived the project of the *Discourse* only in the vagueness of its geographic location. Save that, in the second meditation, methodical doubt leads the philosopher to his window, at least in thought, seeing as in fact he remains seated in his dressing gown, near the fire whose heat he has just famously used to melt a piece of wax: the wax—but doesn't his reasoning apply, by analogy, to the city itself, in the sense in which it is understood in the *Discourse*?—that we think we know through the vision of our eyes, whereas in fact we must resort to what Descartes calls "mental scrutiny" to determine that, after and in spite of its transformation, it remains the same "extended, flexible, and changeable" thing. And Descartes introduces in this connection another comparison that initially seems sophistic:

If by chance I look out of the window and see men crossing the square, I normally say that I see the men themselves, just as I say that I see the wax. And yet, what do I see from the window if not hats and coats that could conceal spectres or automatons? But I *judge* that they are real men. Thus something which I thought I was seeing with my eyes is in fact grasped solely by the faculty of judgment which is in my mind.[2]

The appearance of sophistry here results from the pretense that another's perceptions are an affair of judgment, whereas this comes into play, in the philosopher's view, only when methodical doubt is brought to bear on data obtained through the senses, beginning with sight. Had Descartes indeed considered agitation in the street "by chance," without premeditation, as opposed to going to his window merely in thought, he would not have hesitated, even for an instant, to see men there. But more than a window was needed to justify the incidental introduction of this hypothesis of "human" automata. It is also premised on a plunging perspective view of something like a "street": an element, a configuration, that, while not exclusively urban (even tiny hamlets have house-lined streets), has nonetheless long been considered synonymous with the city, and by metonymy with its population, supposedly uncontrollable ("The government will not surrender to the streets!" was still heard in 1968). From which we extrapolate the following, which pertains to the city itself (whatever one understands this to mean) as well as to its uses and functions, beginning with its philosophical ones: Descartes merely used the city—as Plato did the *polis*—as a concept, a metaphor, or an image. The philosopher was caught, or at least implicated, in his configuration, even if he situated himself within it or made use of it only in thought. And caught, implicated, in several ways. First, in terms of method: the city constituting, explicitly, by way of architecture, a model—and perhaps more than that: a framework of thought privileged with regard to both history and reason—for a philosophy whose constructive intent is acknowledged, one aiming above all "to cast aside loose earth and sand so as to reach [the] rock or clay" that might serve as a solid foundation on which to build.[3] But in conceptual terms as well, if it is true, as Deleuze and Guattari have maintained, that philosophy defines itself first of all as the production of concepts, to which those of Descartes, like the earlier ones of Plato, would not be exceptions: which supposes that one pays attention not only to the forms assumed by this production but also to the sites, real or imaginary, where it occurs and which inevitably resound on the discursive level. I repeat: it was not the countryside and its inhabitants that the philosopher considered in idea, from his window, but a street in which men went about their business; and it was by taking himself in thought to this observation post, itself situated in an artificial milieu, that he was able to feign seeing not men but only hats and cloaks covering spectres or automata. With all the effects that follow from this, in turn, regarding the image of the city, itself considered a kind of machine, one with its own "mechanism" (the time had not yet come to speak of it as a "factory," something from which urbanists circa 1900 would not shy away).

The reference to Descartes is pertinent here because it evidences the establishment, as early as the seventeenth century, of a vision of the city, and of a related set of notions, categories, and oppositions, that remain current in the so-called hour of modernity. This despite the profound transformations that the city itself has undergone in the interim, on the real, imaginary, and symbolic levels. Can the "anarchic" growth of great urban centers be controlled, rationally planned? Can a few discreet interventions suffice to provide cities with the breathing space they so desperately need? And what is the role of architecture in this process? Is it reduced to masking the damage wrought by urban surgery effected without regard for aesthetic considerations, or should it aim—by way of utopian ideals—to be the motor, the inspirational force, at the risk of making matters worse and leading to solutions that are still more radical, and perhaps irreversible? Whether American or "Cartesian" (as Le Corbusier would have it), is the skyscraper the social condenser that the Constructivists thought it to be, or is it, conversely, the surest means of destroying the urban fabric, if it does not presuppose such destruction? Can we still speak of a "city" where the only streets are museum installations, variant forms of the shopping center, or—worse still— double reflections of Disneyland, the city having been reduced to mimicry of its own caricature? Further: Can we judge the image of the future city so insistently impressed upon our minds by the "modern" movement in light of its consequences, which have been derisory on the register of the imaginary, symbolically disastrous, and all too real and universal (although without imputing to architecture itself mistakes resulting from political factors)? Has utopia lost its purchase on the city at the moment when—in the mother of all "deconstructions"—crisis has been substituted, in the way of ineluctable historical horizon, for the revolution it was meant to herald and prepare? Are architects and urbanists reduced to sinning by excess or default, either by imagining gigantic, more or less transformable and ambulatory structures, or, on the contrary, by dreaming of a world freed of all architecture, without bothering themselves (as Colin Rowe has ironically observed) about where, in what subterranean regions, one might house the immense machinery necessary to support a completely artificial human habitat?[4] When, that is, they don't satisfy themselves with repair operations, or with producing urban simulacras inspired by imagery that is exclusively rhetorical, whereas the very idea "city," if it is to retain any meaning, must today entail a refusal, if not of imagery *tout court*, then of all imagery that is resolutely nostalgic or ideological? If we turn our attention to a few questions initially formulated in the late nineteenth century, questions that imply the existence of something called a "history of urbanism" (two words—"history" and "urbanism"—that are problematic in this context, as is a fortiori their conjunction), we immediately grasp the degree to which the opposition, descriptive and generative, posited by Descartes between two types of city has lost none of its currency, including the specific terms he used.

It is one thing, in effect, to regard cities as results of the vicissitudes of time, if not of chance, or as the fruit of a will that, while deliberated, cannot—to follow Descartes—be the work of a single individual, or even of "a few." And it is another to maintain, as the philosopher explicitly does, that the responsibility for building in a preexisting city should fall to architects, whereas the tracing of a town—*place* in its military definition ("post" or "fortress"), which does not necessarily mean "*ville*": the terms here were carefully pondered—on a hitherto completely virginal tract was a task for planners [*ingénieurs*]. But not without, in the absence of a master plan, the imposition of controls designed to guarantee that all such individual constructions "embellish public places." The opposition between architects and engineers, the explicitly marked difference between their respective competences, and the introduction in a third role of administrative agents corresponding to a distinction then operative between the three levels of design (the responsibility of planners [*ingénieurs*]), construction (traditionally overseen by architects), and regulation (enforced by "officers").

One point, however, should be stressed: Descartes may very well, in his fashion, have striven to be "modern," dreaming of placing science and technology in the service of man; even so, he did not advocate the demolition of extant cities so that they could be rebuilt anew. However radical his intentions, however methodical the doubt he brought to bear on traditional ideas, the philosopher did not aim to change the order of the city, nor even its form, its external appearance: the narrator of the *Discourse on the Method* is careful to warn his readers that the project to jettison received opinions so as to build upon a foundation entirely his own was a strictly personal one, and he does not necessarily recommend that others follow his example: just as it is true, he allows, that we never see people tearing down all the houses in a city "for the sole purpose of rebuilding them in a different style," but that we do see individuals demolishing their own when they see fit, sometimes having been obliged to do so because unstable foundations rendered them dangerous.[5] True, the extent of Bramante's Roman projects, and their seemingly chronic incompletion, won him the nickname *maestro ruinante*. But a time would come when architects, claiming technology as their own province and competing, in hopes of prevailing, with the violence of history ("architecture or revolution": such was Le Corbusier's ultimatum), would stipulate a "blank slate" as the premise and first article of their program.

The city would be not only an essential corridor of human history, if not its most remarkable manifestation, as in utopian constructs ("ideal cities"). It would constitute, in its evolution, development, transformations, and countless avatars, a fine paradigm for history, or, to be more precise, a fine model and touchstone for understanding the relation that men maintain with the history that is accounted their own. A history that shapes men more than they shape it, and that easily assumes, with regard to cities, the aspect of a natural history. Certainly this is not the language used by Descartes; in fact, the word *"histoire"* appears in the *Discourse* only in the plural, to designate accounts of memorable actions. And it is worth asking what role utopian constructs could or might have played in a Cartesian context. We know the fantasies, often all too realizable, to which the notion of the "man-machine" has lent itself (and continues to lend itself), in the way of the "scientific" organization of work and, more recently, in the artificial intelligence line. But what, with regard to utopia or the very notion "city," is the status of the Industrial City conceived by Tony Garnier, a century and a half after Ledoux attempted to inscribe on the landscape of Chaux, with the salt factory of the same name, his own image of what Anthony Vidler has called an "architecture of production"?[6]

If the word "history," in the singular, does not figure in Descartes, that is because, unlike Bossuet, the philosopher nowhere perceived traces of a divine plan, and least of all in the city. In the matter of human establishments, the alternative, in the matter of plan, seemed clear. Either we have evolved, with the passage of time, from what were still mere villages to large towns so "ill-proportioned" that it would be tempting to see them as the work of chance alone if officers had not, in all periods, overseen roadways and architects had not taken it upon themselves to embellish them. Or planners were left free to delineate, using ruler and compass, and without taking into account accidents of the terrain, the plan of regular *places* that the text clearly implies should be defined by perpendicular streets (the straight line being an accepted index or symbol of rationality in matters of urbanism); and that without prejudicing their capacity to constitute the kernel or matrix of larger agglomerations, in which "the will of men using reason" would be recognizable. Doubtless there was a dawning awareness in this period that chance has its laws. But Descartes still conceptualized the history of cities in terms that were either strictly formal or purely technical, while positing a clear distinction between these aspects and one that might be called architectural.

Descartes's distinction between these two stages of human agglomeration—the simple town and the large city—leaves unbroached (despite its being raised in the *Discourse*) the question of the city's future, and first of its definition, of what the city as such is or could be. From what moment in this process of becoming can we rightly speak of a "city," large or small, as opposed to a village or a town? Further: Beyond what point is the city threatened in its form and functioning, in its definition, its identity, its very being as "city"? If we attempt to judge these matters in strictly quantitative terms, above all demographic ones, we soon find ourselves confronting a paradox analogous to the ones that so delighted the Eleatic philosophers: What is the minimal threshold, in an accumulation of grains of sand, beyond which we can speak of a "pile" of sand, and what is the upper limit beyond which this designation no longer applies? At what point, when a man is losing his hair, can he be described as "bald"? How many trees must there be before we can speak of a "forest"? Similarly, from what point, and until what upper limit, can we speak of a "city"? The problem being, for example, to determine what notion of the city Descartes could have sustained, beyond the essentially constructive image he imposes on it at the beginning of the *Discourse*; a discourse, it bears repeating, on method, not on history.

In this connection, still pertaining to Descartes, if not to all of philosophy, Adrien Baillet reports the following about his residence, his habitat—the residence and habitat of Descartes; but also that of philosophy such as he thought it should be practiced:

Although [Descartes] prided himself on being able to retain his solitude in the largest crowds as well as in the depths of the desert, he nonetheless avoided the heart of large cities, preferring to lodge at the farthest extremity of their suburbs. He always preferred villages and detached houses in the middle of the countryside, when comfortable ones could be found close enough to cities such that he could easily draw his subsistence from them.[7]

Bodily subsistence as much—one is tempted to suggest, at least in terms of image—as subsistence for the intellect, if not for philosophy, as evidenced by his desire to remain on the outskirts of large agglomerations ("at the farthest extremity of their suburbs"), or at least within their immediate proximity. As though the city were all the more present to his mind, all the more active, all the more nourishing, in its double capacity as reservoir of metaphors and dispenser of concepts, insofar as he affected (and was inclined) to keep himself at a convenient distance from its center, so as to make use of it only in the realm of ideas—and of images.

The city conceptualized from its center, or, conversely, from its margins, from its outskirts and perimeter. These same outskirts, these same suburbs whose ongoing extension today raises different questions about the nature of urban agglomerations, about their growth and aspect; as if the boundary once made concrete by city walls had become porous and thus compromised the center's dominance, with the suburbs now effectively thriving as parasites on the city: the city as place of residence, work, subsistence, and commerce; but also as a site of diversion, as a concatenation of pleasures. To say nothing of the megalopolis, as opposed to the metropolis, proliferating agglomerations in which the relation between center and periphery seems to be reversed, when the very idea of centrality has not become utterly irrelevant. Doubtless all views of the city current in our own time are tributaries, in one way or another, of the perspective configuration—perspective being essentially constructive, if not urban.[8] But in these images the subject is no longer implicated as in frontal views: traditional *vedute* and depictions of rooftop silhouettes have given way to bird's-eye views. A century and a half after Brunelleschi perfected the first "urban perspectives," Jacques Callot engraved the same sites exploited by the Florentine architect in his experiments—the Piazza della Signoria, the Piazza San Giovanni—but introduced into the corner of his compositions, in the position of the observer, a figure on an artificial hill taking in the spectacle of the city offered by his elevated perch. However crude in iconographic terms, this procedure nonetheless evidences a concern to obtain—and to present—a more comprehensive vision of the city. The strictly horizontal view provided by the little

hole pierced at the location of the vanishing point, through which
Brunelleschi invited the spectator to consider the image in a mirror,
has been replaced by a downward view from above, with as corollary another kind of distance than the one implicated by the initial
configuration: the observer is no longer immediately implicated in
the spectacle, being positioned at eye-level and at a reasonable proximity, as with Brunelleschi. Rather, he is moved simultaneously backward and upward.

Long before the invention of the airplane, men of art were able
to obtain, largely through graphic means, "bird's-eye views," the image of the city being confounded with its maquette, its relief plan.
But such a vision of the city was not an exclusively iconographic
matter. In all periods, the city has trained its gaze on itself, at eye-
level, along its streets and squares, or from the top of towers offering plunging views. When the time came, in the seventeenth century, with its carefully constructed "perspectives" (some displaying
the city's interior, others abstracting it, shifting instead toward its exterior), the bird's-eye view would assert itself, making it possible to
assess its effects. But only in the nineteenth century did architects
multiply panoramic prospects by erecting all manner of belvederes
and terraces, bridges, viaducts, elevated trains, and, before long,
towers on a scale quite other from those of the medieval period.
Does the city remain "real" when considered from such distances, as
a spectacle, a scene, and ultimately as a stage set, a backdrop?[9] It is as
though, at the moment when the great city, the metropolis, the
Grossstadt, was beginning to call for an image of agglomeration other
than a strictly architectural one, it seemed indispensable to preserve
its visibility or, to evoke a Freudian problematic, its *representability*.

It is remarkable that architects strove to view the city as a work
of art, in the sense that Marx spoke of manufacture as "an economic
work of art,"[10] but succeeded in doing so only by cleansing it, in
imagination, of its population. If there is a utopian version of the
"industrial city," it would result from an operation like the one effected, in the order of representation, by a photographer such as Eu-
gène Atget in his views of a Paris emptied, to this end, of its inhabi-

tants. With the difference, a significant one, that while the absence of all humanity confers on the image of the industrial city as conceived by Tony Garnier an incomparable clarity, Atget's photographs of Paris, avoiding as they do encompassing views to concentrate at close proximity on fugitive details and repetitive elements of the urban site, reveal, as in a photographic negative, its dark ground. It is not without reason, observed Walter Benjamin, that Atget's views have been compared to stage photography: "But is not every square inch of our cities the scene of a crime? Every passer-by a criminal?"[11]

Two centuries after Descartes, fiction would open onto the street a window quite different from the one in the *Meditations*, although one that still left mischievous genius the freedom to exercise its gifts, if in other ways and to different effect. The same Walter Benjamin discerned in the writing of Edgar Allan Poe a classic description of the crowd in the modern sense, which began to crystallize precisely when Poe was writing. A crowd very different from the "largest crowd of people" in which, if we can believe Baillet, Descartes took pride in being able to "retain his solitude," although throngs, sometimes violent ones, were not unknown in the seventeenth-century city. A crowd that certainly no longer lent itself, animated as it was, to mechanist interpretations, but solicited first of all close observation of its slightest movement. A crowd through which some easily made their way, whereas others seemed agitated and uneasy, "as if feeling in solitude on account of the very denseness of the company around."[12] The crowd functioning in Poe, like the mob in Baudelaire, as a magnetic field that, quite often, is the silent consort of the individuals that Benjamin called *flâneurs*, a type characteristic of large nineteenth-century cities. The same solitude that Baudelaire loved, but that he sought out in the crowd (whereas Descartes only accommodated himself to it): a crowd in which the poet saw "the newest drug for the solitary" as well as "the newest asylum for the reprobate,"[13] for those who refused to be alone, as we read in Poe. As Benjamin rightly noted, the primitive social content of detective stories (beginning with those of Edgar Allan Poe) is the obliteration of the individual's traces in the crowds endemic to large cities, for example on the famous Parisian "Boulevard du Crime," with its many theaters. But the narrator of "The Man of the Crowd" attaches himself not only to the strange old man that he pursues in the light of street lamps, until the moment he recognizes in him, in Poe's words, "the type and the genius of deep crime." He first takes the time to examine the crowd as mass and in detail, from the observation post assigned him by the modern city: not the window of an apartment overlooking a dark alley but the large bow window of a coffeehouse on one of London's main thoroughfares.

The question of the visibility of the city, or—as we would now say—of its "legibility," if not its "representability," became pressing only from the moment its image was unsettled, not only as a result of the ever more apparent divorce between the forms and functions generally regarded as its own, but also because of the dissolution of traditional communitarian ties in the midst of the mob. The same mob—to cite Benjamin on Baudelaire—that is, "within the labyrinth of the city, the masses are the newest and most inscrutable labyrinth. Through them previously unknown chthonic traits are imprinted on the image of the city."[14] As we shall see in the next chapter, the example of the Egyptian labyrinth described by Herodotus is enlightening in this regard: beyond certain spatial or merely numerical limits, and however clear and regular its plan, every built structure lends itself to multiple traversals that are themselves labyrinthine. What Benjamin retained from Poe and Baudelaire is the notion that, beyond a certain critical mass, the paths traced by the man of the city, by the man of the crowd, effectively evoke the illegible, indecipherable figure of a labyrinth whose subterranean presence will obliterate the image of the city all the more insofar as the latter is homogenous and extended.

Windows are always only one of the many gazes that the city opens onto itself. But a privileged gaze insofar as it is singular, individual, *private*, and one through which not only the street but also the labyrinth of the city can erupt into the space in which the subject resides. It is one thing for Descartes, meditating in the calm of a well-heated room, to take himself in thought to the nearest window. And it is another for the narrator of "The Man of the Crowd" to find himself implicated in the animation of public spaces where architecture organizes, through the interplay of circulation routes, of transparencies and reflections, what Poe calls "the scene without" (translated by Baudelaire as "*la scène du dehors*"). With the risk that this scene, this *dehors*, but also this lack ("without"), might solicit the spectator, tempting him ceaselessly to throw himself into the street and lose himself in the crowd. For the drift to which the air, movement, and even noises of the city expose the modern subject is not, or is no longer, an affair of either perspective or point of view, nor of judgment. Even if he remains in his lodging, the mere opening of a window can provoke in him an overflow that literally flings him outside of himself.

Baudelaire recounts a striking example of the "nervous jokes" —according to him, sometimes termed "hysterical" and sometimes "satanic"—occasionally perpetrated by individuals whose natures are dreamy and contemplative. When the narrator of *Le Spleen de Paris* opens his window one morning and hears, through the "thick, oppressive Parisian air," the cry of an itinerant artisan, the sound triggers a fit of destructive madness, prompting him to summon the poor glazier to his garret and then, after having sent him away again, to drop a flowerpot on him that shatters all his merchandise, ostensibly because the man had not been carrying any colored glass that would have made it possible for the narrator and other residents of his impoverished neighborhood to see "life as beautiful." The fable of the "Bad Glazier" makes it clear that windows had lost their value as signs and instruments of a mastery of the outside, a function they sometimes assume in classic thought in the guise of views or *tableaux* that are well framed, considered from the right distance. Instead, as sites where interior meets exterior, where inside meets outside, they function as emblems or symbols of circulating flux, of the physical, drive-based impulses characteristic of large cities, whose glass is unable to filter out external violence. The subject (who here, as in Baudelaire and already in Descartes, speaks in the first person) no longer finding it possible to remain in the background, behind his window and in the position of the observer, just as he is unable to dispose as he likes, in thought, of the spectacle of the street. The city (the "street") is there, it unceremoniously forces upon him its indiscreet, even "chthonic" presence (as Benjamin would have it).

Neither the difficulty experienced by anyone who tries to speak objectively about the city, nor, conversely, the vividness of literary testimony about it,[15] implies that all discourse about the city and relations to it, as well as all images or visions of it, must be subjective. Rather, these circumstances reflect the fact that cities have always been privileged sites, if in guises that are constantly changing, for interrogating the nature of the subject, for investigating just what markers it needs to keep its bearings in the milieu within which it is evolving: sites, if not of the emergence of the very question of the subject in the modern, Cartesian sense of the word, then at least of its conceptual articulation in terms of its relations to history and to other persons. It is impossible to reduce the city to an object, unless the subject envisions it, through another's perceptions, as a "machine," thereby simultaneously excluding itself from the configuration of address [*dispositif d'énonciation*] that is the very condition of discourse: paradoxically, the solitude to which inhabitants of large cities and endless suburbs are exposed is scarcely conducive to solipsism. But it is likewise impossible to accept an image of the polis, defined as a community of free subjects, that would solicit an urban form precisely suited to its founding project. With the *Grosstadt*, not to mention the megalopolis, we are far from the ancient city, but we are just as far from the classic city, and from machinist reveries and industrial utopias.

The opposition posited by Descartes between an urban evolution that is virtually spontaneous and one that is more or less controlled, and perhaps the result of comprehensive planning, does not do justice to the multiplicity and intricacy of the causes that, historically speaking, led to the appearance of large cities, ancient and modern. Unlike the philosopher's piece of wax, the city is irreducible to something extended, flexible, and infinitely changeable. The city is not a thing, nor can it be restored to some basic substance.

But when analyzing the city as an object, how can we take the human element into account in terms other than numerical ones, or, at the opposite extreme, in the form of "life stories" such as were favored by the Chicago school of sociology?[16] And how can events, as well as local initiatives and decisions taken by social agents, be integrated into a determinist model of urban evolution? For all their sophistication, paradigms derived from game theory, thermodynamics, and artificial intelligence come to grief at the same point: just as progress in our biological understanding of the brain does not invalidate philosophical approaches to mind and consciousness,[17] advances in urban analysis do not preclude reflection on the notion, the concept, even the very idea of the "city," and on the representations linked to it in the Western imagination.

We cannot, in effect, be satisfied with an ethnocentric brand of phenomenology fed by images of the European city in literature and iconography, and at the same time privilege conscious ways of approaching the urban phenomenon. Just short of three centuries after Descartes, Freud had recourse to the metaphor of the city to clarify, at the beginning of *Civilization and Its Discontents*, by way of clarifying the difference between the archaeology of what he called "the soul" ("*die Seele*") and that of the city—ancient Rome—which Western culture boldly refers to as "eternal": as if the idea of the city —and with it, that of civilization—pervasive in European thought could have meaning, ultimately, only if abstracted from the hazards of time (in Spengler's view, the decline of the West was inseparable from that of the city). Now the problem confronting (psycho)analysts of the city might be the precise opposite of the one articulated by Freud: for them, it is less a question of clarifying the life of the "soul" (if not of the mind) through recourse to visual images than of appealing to the paradoxical temporality of the unconscious while trying to account for the spatial evolution of the city. If it is true, as Freud maintained, that the unconscious has no history and does not want to know that it is mortal, it nonetheless retains traces of all the successive stages of psychic life, as well as of all the events and experiences constituting it. It is up to the subject to give first-person narrative, or historical, form to this dark ground that it can know only through scraps and figures, and whose return, whose surfacing, whose emergence into the light eludes all conscious control.

Doubtless the history of cities is subject to very different determinations, if only because the construction of new buildings presupposes the demolition of those previously occupying the same site, whereas the unconscious can easily accommodate the survival of archaic formations beside others that have supplanted them, even on the same site. Hence the difference between the characteristics of mental life (the "soul") and those of the visual images (as well as the mechanical, biological, and digital models) through which we attempt to comprehend them. As Freud wrote, "If we want to represent historical sequence in spatial terms we can only do it by juxtaposition in space: the same space cannot have two different contents."[18]

Even so, the city is no stranger to operations of a kind specific to the unconscious. Derisory attempts to build new urban complexes that are "predigested" and that, like prewashed jeans, already have the patina of age, can have no effect on the "collage" of heterogeneous elements whose function in urban contexts is analogous to those of displacement and condensation in dreams, telescoping the past and the present.[19] For, even on the level of form, it comes to one and the same thing to claim that the sole reality of cities is historical and to maintain that they exist only in the present.[20] Much the same holds for the unconscious, which likewise can manifest itself overtly only in the present, in ways that have no immediately discernible resemblance to a palimpsest. So we should not be surprised that, contemporary with the transformation of the classical city into the *Grosstadt*, there was an evolution from the city as figure in a discourse on method to the city as figure in a discourse on the unconscious: a matter, in both cases, of *Darstellbarkeit*, of *representability*, more than of vision.

Between Descartes and Freud, the relation between thought and its habitat was radically transformed, as indicated by the familiar image of the repressed that, chased out the door, returns through

the window. But via what routes, what detours? Which raises another question: What difference does it make to the unconscious
whether it roams the countryside or lets itself be caught in the city,
in its mazes, in its labyrinth? This prompts another question, one
that might serve as a preamble to all reflection bearing not only on
representations of the city but also on the spatial positioning of the
subject: Can we imagine the fable of Narcissus taking place in an
urban context? To put this differently: What would an urban Narcissus be like, how would he differ from the Narcissus of fields,
woods, and springs? To what forms, to what modalities of narcis-
sism—they must relate in some way to the vision of the city accessible to him—is the city-dweller reduced? Conversely, what funda-
mentally narcissistic structure is specific to the urban context as well
as to its inhabitants and its users? What kind of gaze does the city
license? To rephrase: What kind of gaze does it induce, determine,
inform, program, organize? What kind of gaze, not only is the subject able to turn on itself, but does the city-machine turn on itself
through the intermediary of the said "subject"? What is the nature,
indissolubly, of the city as reality, as image, and as symbol? What is
this object of desire, at once near and ungraspable, fascinating and
repulsive, attractive and intractable, necessary and unbearable, intimate and impenetrable, available and inaccessible, that it is for itself as well as for the man of the crowd, for the man in the street,
for the man of the city, for those who inhabit it and those merely
passing through it, for anyone who knows that it is a labyrinth but
nonetheless allows himself to remain trapped in it?

2

The Egyptian Labyrinth

For Pierre Rosenstiehl

As Herodotus describes it very near the end of Book II of his *History*, the Egyptian labyrinth is perfectly consistent with his observation that, of all the countries known to him, Egypt seemed to contain the most marvels, being possessed of, as he put it, "more works that are beyond description than any other"[1]: the comparison being based from the start on grounds of language and related to measures that are those of discourse. Thus he proceeds from the edifice he was able to visit, at least in part, beside the Lake of Moeris and some miles from the city the Greeks named Crocodilopolis, "City of the Crocodiles," the ancient Shadit, the Arsinoé of the Ptolemaic period, the ancient capital of Fayoum whose ruins are to the north of Médinet el-Fayoum.[2] "I saw it myself," we read in the *History*,

and it is indeed a wonder past words; for if one were to collect together all the buildings of the Greeks and their most striking works of architecture, they would all clearly be shown to have cost less labor and money than this labyrinth. Yet the temple at Ephesus and that in Samos are surely remarkable. The pyramids, too, were greater than words could tell, and each of them is the equivalent of many of the great works of the Greeks; but the labyrinth surpasses the pyramids also.[3]

At first glance, Herodotus's description of this singular edifice is difficult to reconcile with the conventional notion of a "labyrinth": a complex network of galleries or corridors from which anyone who ventures beyond a certain point will be unable to find his way out unless he has left behind a string enabling him to retrace his steps. Should we be surprised by this, given that, according to the author of the *History*:

Just as the climate that the Egyptians have is entirely their own and different from anyone else's, and their river has a nature quite different from other rivers, so, in fact, the most of what they have made their habits and their customs are the exact opposite of other folks.[4]

From there to presenting as a labyrinth an edifice apparently lacking all of the features characteristic of such a structure, there was more than one step that Herodotus did not hesitate to make, any more than he hesitated to enter this mysterious place. And what do we read, in effect, still in Book II of the *History*? That this *laburinthos* consisted of twelve roofed and contiguous courts surrounded by a single enclosing wall and disposed, apparently, in two rows with aligned doors, six to the south and six to the north. Furthermore (we will see that this feature is significant), the roof of these structures was made of stone, as were the walls, the latter being covered with "engraved figures," while each of the courts was surrounded by "very exactly fitted" pillars of white stone. Which amounts to a configuration that is, in itself, not the least bit disorienting and even less chaotic, if we discount its redoubled immensity. "There are," Herodotus continues,

double sets of chambers in it, some underground and some above, and their number is three thousand; there are fifteen hundred of each. We ourselves saw the aboveground chambers, for we went through them and so can talk of them, but the underground chambers we can speak of only from hearsay. For the officials of the Egyptians entirely refused to show us these, saying that there were, in them, the coffins of the kings who had builded the labyrinth at the beginning and also those of the holy crocodiles. So we speak from hearsay of these underground places; but what we saw aboveground was certainly greater than all human works.[5]

As the French translator of Herodotus observes, he here delights in underscoring that he was allowed to enter the labyrinth, whereas ordinarily he could view the Egyptian buildings he describes only from the outside. But the interior of the labyrinth nonetheless figures in this last part of Book II of the *History*, where Herodotus notes that, contrary to his practice up to that point, he would not confine himself to what he saw and information that he had gathered, any more than to stories the Egyptians had told him about their country's history: on the verge of applying the finishing touches to his picture, he has yet to give an account of "what other men and the Egyptians say in agreement as having happened in this country,"[6] but not without adding something that he himself had observed. And although he indeed saw, with his own eyes, the upper rooms of the labyrinth (insofar as a labyrinth is something accessible to vision, something that solicits the gaze, something that can be seen, observed, or contemplated: matters to which we shall return), he could speak of the underground rooms only by hearsay, the information he had managed to obtain about them (or should we say: without them?) having been limited to the following: that their disposition apparently repeated that of the rooms above ground. But as to what "other men" could know or think about them, this question is inextricable from another, that of the very meaning of "labyrinth."

Strabo agrees with Herodotus in regarding the Egyptian labyrinth as a work comparable to the pyramids. According to him, the structures of lesser dimensions apparently constituting what he called "this great palace" were equal in number to the administrative divisions of ancient Egypt, the reason being, as he was told, that it was customary for their representatives to assemble in this place, according to rank, with their priests, to sacrifice to the gods and render justice in important matters, each group having first been led to their designated court. Surrounded by columns, these courts were indeed "contiguous," as Herodotus had reported previously, but were disposed, according to Strabo, in a single row along a wall to which the access routes were perpendicular. Opposite the entrance of each of these courts there opened long and numerous cryptlike structures composed of twisting passages communicating with one another such that no stranger could find his way through them without the aid of a guide, whether to enter one of the courts or to leave it, the labyrinth proper having been relegated to the periphery. But the most remarkable thing, according to Strabo, was that the roof of each room consisted of a single stone, as with the crypts, each being covered by a slab of enormous dimensions, without recourse to beams or any other material:

Climbing up to the roof, which was not very high as the labyrinth consisted of a single story, one thought one saw a plain of stone, composed of blocks of large dimensions. And, redescending to the courts, one saw that they were aligned, each one being supported by twenty-seven monolithic pillars, their walls being made of stones that were not of lesser dimensions.[7]

That the Egyptians, liberated after the reign of one he describes as a priest of Hephaestus, had decided, according to Herodotus, to create a dozen kings and divide Egypt into a dozen corresponding kingdoms, and then built a monument common to all of them, in the guise of a labyrinth featuring twelve courts, this assertion is not necessarily at odds with the fact that the dodecarchy organized in Lower Egypt had given way, before Psammetichus, to multiple little kings, some allied among themselves and others enemies of one another.[8] Given this context, the purpose of the monument described by Herodotus might have been not only administrative but also political, even ideological, constituting an image of a society that, while not unified, was nonetheless reconciled with itself. But, conceptually as well as architecturally, such a structure would still be far from the generally accepted notion of a "labyrinth."

Pliny saw the problem so clearly that he sought to circumvent it through slight of hand, introducing into the *Natural History* something that is clearly a mistake. Although Herodotus seems to have been the first Greek author to employ the term "labyrinth," using it to describe the great complex at Hawara by analogy with what he knew about the palace of Minos and its confusing plan, Pliny maintains that Daedalus took the Egyptian complex as a model for the labyrinth he built in Crete, reducing it, says Pliny, to one-hundredth the size of the original and appending double galleries with inextricable twists and turns. To which were added numerous doors designed to trick the visitor and repeatedly lead him back to the same dead ends. He also asserts that a third labyrinth was built later in Lemnos, followed by another in Clusium, in Etruria, both with vaults of polished stone,[9] and that the entrance and columns of the Egyptian labyrinth were made of Parian marble—a surprising observation, if, like Pliny, we take it literally. "The rest is composed of blocks of syenite joined together, which the centuries themselves would not be able to break asunder, even with the aid of the Heracleopolitans, who singularly ravaged a work that they detested."[10]

There follows, in Book XXXVI of the *Natural History*, a description of this despised object that merits citation in its entirety:

It is not possible to describe in detail the position of this monument nor its different parts; it is divided into regions and districts called "nomes," whose twenty-one names are attributed to as many vast residences; it also contains temples to all the gods of Egypt. Furthermore, Nemesis has enclosed in forty small edifices numerous pyramids forty brasses high and each occupying at the base a surface of six "aroures." One is already exhausted from walking when one reaches an inextricable network of routes, then again on upper, elevated stories accessible by stairs, and one descends the porticos by stairs with ninety steps. Inside, one finds porphyry columns, effigies of the gods, statues of kings, representations of monsters. Some residences are constructed such that when the doors open terrible thunderclaps sound from within. And most of their traversal takes place in darkness. There are, furthermore, other masses of buildings within the wall of the labyrinth; they form what is called the *pteron*. Then some galleries excavated in the ground give birth to underground halls. Chaeremon, eunuch of King Necthebis, was the only one to make some repairs there, fifty years before Alexander the Great. Tradition also says that beams of mimosa boiled in oil were used to reinforce the vaults that were built of dressed stone.[11]

It will be easier to grasp just how surprising this description is if we attend to the transition, much like Pliny's (which, I repeat, seems to be a deliberate lapse), by which we pass from the labyrinth of Lemnos to the one in Italy: *Et de Creticoi labyrintho satis dictum est*, "But enough has been said about the Cretan labyrinth."[12] How can Pliny express himself in such terms when the preceding description pertains not to the Cretan labyrinth but to that of Egypt, of which the first must have been a copy or a reduction? Doubtless this phrase is an indication—unintended by Pliny—that his description was directly informed, programmed, and even contaminated by the Cretan example. Daedalus might indeed have taken the Egyptian labyrinth as his model, reproducing it on a smaller scale and, apparently, making its plan more complex. But Pliny nonetheless used the mythical labyrinth as his point of reference in revising the traditional description of the Egyptian labyrinth, which was divided into as many parts as Egypt had nomes (the number of which Pliny increases to twenty-one), projecting onto the regular configuration described by his predecessors the chaotic image of the Minotaur's lair. Not content with multiplying, as in Jorge Luis Borges's City of the Immortals, levels and stairways, ascending and descending routes of every variety, the author of the *Natural History* introduces into his scenario two additional features. First, a soundtrack, in the guise of thunderclaps intended to frighten lost visitors. And second—a feature left implicit by both Herodotus and Strabo—a calculated absence of light: the underground rooms, crypts, and galleries are of course plunged into darkness, but this also reigns in the upper parts of the edifice, covered as they are by stone slabs.

Thus everything suggests that Pliny had grasped the problem arising from use of the word "labyrinth" to designate the complex at Hawara, and that he set out to resolve the difficulty, more or less deliberately, by reducing the conceptual discrepancies between the image of a rationally conceived architectural configuration whose extent and monotony nonetheless gave it a traplike aspect,[14] and that of the mythical labyrinth, whose intricacy was apparently intended to compensate for its smaller dimensions. (But if the Egyptian labyrinth exceeded all human measure, would Daedalus's supposed reduction of it to $1/100$th of its original size have sufficed to give the Cretan example a human scale? In the matter of labyrinths, can man serve as the measure?) Not to mention that in Herodotus, as in Strabo's later text, the image of the Egyptian labyrinth is shorn of all narrative connotations, being situated toward the end of the extended parenthesis that constitutes, in the course of the *Natural History*, the description of Egypt.

No narrative connotations, any more than agonistic ones (Pliny's description retaining only a single feature redolent of the Cretan labyrinth's inhabitant: the depictions of monsters on the walls of the Egyptian structure). As to the mythical labyrinth, Theseus would not have gone to Crete merely to visit it. Once inside, getting out was not the only problem that confronted him: first he had to find and slay the Minotaur. As to the hero's ability to prevail in the encounter, this was not subject to doubt. The latter task having been completed, however, he had to renegotiate the labyrinth, something he managed to do only with Ariadne's help, using a strategy devised by Daedalus himself. In effect, the hero's destiny hung, literally, by a thread. As for Daedalus, imprisoned in the labyrinth for having assisted Theseus, he managed to escape only by renouncing the idea of retracing his steps in favor of taking to the air, but even this act did not afford him a comprehensive view of the whole. Pliny, like Herodotus and Strabo before him, pointedly informs his readers that the ancient labyrinths were roofed, thus rendering moot all thought of a revelatory overhead view.[15]

Thus Theseus's principal adversary was not the Minotaur but the labyrinth itself, considered as the site or support of a game with two possible outcomes. It was not enough for the hero, having found the beast, to annihilate it, his fate otherwise having been to be devoured, one of the possible outcomes. After killing the Minotaur, he had to find his way out of the labyrinth, the game requiring a double, in-and-out movement. Completion of the first task, locating and dispatching the Minotaur, hinged on Theseus's being able to explore every nook and cranny of the labyrinth; that of the second required—such was the premise of the expedient of Ariadne's thread —that he retrace his initial course precisely, detours and all. The confrontation of the two hostile parties could have brought the story to an end: being contained by the topography of the labyrinth and subject to its own constraints, the duel between man and beast, like the confrontation of black and white pieces in a chess match, required of each player that he adopt a strategy of his own. Admittedly, while every move in a game of chess is devised to foil that of one's opponent, the monster was incapable of devising a strategy; but the labyrinth itself—although it might seem to have been made by other than human hands, insofar as its measure could not be taken by language—was the result of a concerted strategy: a strategy of confusion, disorder, and disorientation designed both to keep the monster prisoner and to lead astray anyone trying to confront it.

The Egyptian labyrinth is not associated with any story in ancient literature, nor with any ancient ritual or mythic function. And it is difficult to see, at first reading, what might have led Herodotus to use the word "labyrinth" to designate something that was perhaps a temple, or a palace, or even a complex of administrative buildings that tourists could visit. However questionable the designation, and Pliny seems to have been aware of the attendant problems, it finds some justification on the level of discourse. The description of the Egyptian labyrinth is articulated within two time frames and operates on two distinct levels. First, on the level of the object, the labyrinth being presented as an architectural complex that the historian was able to see and even visit, a structure that he attempted to describe but that, to an even greater extent than the pyramids, eluded discursive capture ("kai erga logou mezó"), just as it exceeded ("uperballei") in its size all the works produced by the Greeks. But exceeded them—since it exceeded anything that might be said about it—in terms that were not exclusively quantitative. Its dimensions, its extent, its very enormity implying a qualitative leap. As Herodotus observes, even if one were to add up all the works of the Greeks, one would have been unable to obtain, by simple addition, the labyrinth, which resulted from an operation of another order, one aiming at effects other than demonstrative ones (as indicated by use of the word *apodeixis* in connection with the architectural production of the Greeks). Although qualitative, the leap in question pertains both to the object itself and to the discourse intended to describe it: considered as a *cosa mentale*, as an object of discourse, the Egyptian labyrinth corresponded to a kind of squaring-the-circle limit case implicating both rhetoric and logic.

Situated as it is at the end of a book wholly devoted to the description of a country rich in works that defy comprehension (to such an extent that they do not seem to be human constructions), the description of the Egyptian labyrinth clearly has rhetorical connotations. Even so, Herodotus does not limit himself to the notion, hyperbolic for a Greek, of a building regular in plan but so enormous and repetitive that anyone venturing inside without a guide becomes lost. For in a second moment, on a second level of description, the *built* maze of the labyrinth is replaced by the seemingly endless maze of routes actually taken:

The passages through the rooms and the winding goings-in and out through the courts, in their extreme complication, caused us countless marvelings as we went through, from the court into the rooms, and from the rooms into the pillared corridors, and then from these corridors into other rooms again, and from the rooms into other courts afterwards.[17]

In other words, if there is indeed question of a "labyrinth" here, it corresponds less to the building itself than to the seemingly infinite, inscrutable network of itineraries inscribable within it, and which stand out against this dark ground like a negative, or like the "engraved figures" on the walls (whereas Daedalus was thought to have invented both the labyrinth and the freestanding *statue* independent of architectural context). In the matter of labyrinths, that of Egypt is primarily one of meandering paths and detours, whose sinuous turns are echoed by the dance performed by Theseus's companions after his escape from the labyrinth.[18] Detours and turns as complex ("oi eiligmoi polikilôtatoi") as the folds of the intestine, the interlaces of a knot, or the changeable, entangled paths taken by guile to achieve its ends.

The image of the labyrinth is, then, closely linked to the cunning that the Greeks called *métis*, a form of intelligence whose secret, obsessive presence Marcel Detienne and Jean-Pierre Vernant have discerned, between the lines, throughout Hellenic culture. Like an octopus with a thousand arms, the labyrinth is a kind of *poikilos*, a disorienting place whose tentacular passages extend in all directions.[19] Something analogous to the burrows with multiple entrances where foxes lurk and hatch their schemes: the same foxes that play dead the better to spring on their victims; animals that incarnate cunning, being experts at reversal, masters of entrapment like the octopus, which nothing can encompass but which can lay hold of anything.[20] Admittedly, the regular, rectilinear disposition of the courts of the Egyptian labyrinth is not at all consistent with the image of a network of interlaced tentacles (*poluplokos*, a word used to describe octopuses, snakes, and labyrinths). Nevertheless, this building with none of the characteristic features of classical Greek architecture, this edifice lacking facade and forecourt, profile and contour, without a "skyline," and whose external aspect reveals nothing of its internal structure or plan, comprehensible only after the fact, and whose very ruins allow of only hypothetical reconstruction, this design whose sole exterior feature is a continuous wall, this architecture wholly "internal," almost visceral, immersed as it is for the most part—and, in the underground rooms, entirely —in darkness, shares many qualities with cephalopods, octopuses, and cuttlefish, notably with the inky night in which they envelope themselves to elude their enemies and entrap their victims:

Oblique animals whose fronts are never readily distinguishable from their backs, they confound, in their bearing and their physical being, all directions. Cuttlefish and octopuses are pure aporias, and the night that they secrete, a night without issue, without pathways, is the most complete expression of their *métis*. In this profound darkness, cuttlefish and octopuses are the only ones able to find their way, to open a *poros* for themselves.[21]

But the labyrinth of Egypt is also cunning in that, on the descriptive level, it presents itself as being other than it is, its regular design having been contrived to mislead anyone who dared enter it without authorization, without an accompanying guide. Its entrance (an entrance, not a facade) and its countless regularly arrayed interior columns would have seemed familiar to Greeks and Romans, so much so that Pliny supposed them made of Parian marble. The symmetrical distribution of the courts was apparent to him only after the fact, as he never obtained a view of the whole, the rectilinear disposition of the porticos having been contrived to reassure the visitor, soon disabused by the many windings and detours, by the profusion of all manner of false trails and dead ends. The Egyptian complex presented all the characteristic features of a labyrinth in terms of plan, despite its structural dissimilarity from the Cretan labyrinth. Analogously (and the difference is important), whereas in Egypt guides were made available to visitors, Daedalus himself was ignorant of the plan of the labyrinth he had conceived, resorting of necessity to cunning as a means of enabling Theseus to negotiate it and, after completion of his mission, to foil—without definitively resolving—the aporia, to relocate the exit, the *poros*.

Cunning could be outwitted only by cunning that was subtler still, that took it as a model the better to one-up its tricks. To catch cuttlefish, fishermen used females of the same species as bait, for their fellow creatures gripped them with such force that nothing could weaken it save death.[22] The "law" of *métis* stipulated, in effect, that a *polumètos* could be defeated only by being more *métis* than its opponent. But the means were strictly programmed: according to the Greeks, only like was effective against like. To prevail, a crafty person had to turn his enemy's own weapons against him, in the way that Sophists used the arguments of their opponents. Such was the strategy adopted by Daedalus, who was a master of cunning: unable to provide Theseus with a plan, the architect of the labyrinth made it possible for him to avoid capture in its snare by providing him with a string that would marry his winding course, a ruse making it possible for him to retrace his steps precisely.

Taking Daedalus's trick as their model, mathematicians are now trying to convince us that, with a little method, we should be able to extract ourselves from any labyrinthine situation.[23] Since the golden rule for such extraction stipulates that one must never proceed down the same passage twice in the same direction, an exhaustive traversal would entail the visitor's proceeding down each passage precisely twice, once in each direction. Theseus would have been obliged to undertake an exploration of precisely this kind: only an exhaustive traversal would have guaranteed an encounter with the Minotaur. But this same rule would have made it possible for Daedalus, thrown as he was into the labyrinth, to escape from it by leaving behind him marks of some sort on the ground or the walls, at the entrance or exit of corridors he had already taken, substitutes for the thread that was not available to him (a solution premised, let it be noted, on the labyrinth's not having been completely dark, or on Daedalus's having been equipped with a lantern, for otherwise he would have been reduced to an exclusively tactile exploration).

Labyrinths on a single level would be traps, then, only for visitors who, proceeding without any such method, were reduced to wandering aimlessly, making haphazard decisions at each point without paying any attention to what routes they had taken previously, knowing nothing of the algebraic structures that govern the linear traversal of all surfaces and that make it possible, by means of *analysis situs*, of algebraic topology, for someone to orient himself within such a network of intersections. The important thing still being, given the absence of any overall plan (standard for labyrinths, save after the fact), that the reckoner will be reduced, at every point, to making use solely of local givens: when plotting the course of a line on a graph algebraically, one can exploit comprehensive data analogous to a bird's-eye view, whereas a labyrinth presents itself from the start not merely as a network, but as a situation in which no algorithm will be applicable that is not itself *myopic* and consistent with local data.

"It is the traveler and his myopia who makes the labyrinth, not the architect and his perspectives."[24] The traveler and his myopia (supposing, as before, that he can see); but also the desire that prompts him, in the absence of any specific mission (destroying the beast), to explore the place thoroughly, inclusive of all detours and recesses, as economically as possible, expending the minimum amount of time and energy necessary to do so. But the game (the desire) of the labyrinth would not be worth a candle (an item whose importance has already been emphasized) if there were no risk of confusion. Confusion prompted by fear of being unable to relocate the exit; but confusion, furthermore, linked to a limitation imposed on vision: short-sightedness, or myopia, tends to foster the loss of one's way insofar as it is a parameter of the labyrinthine situation.

Now we are better placed to see the typological problem raised by the Egyptian labyrinth. And *see* is indeed the appropriate word here, as what is in question is a building that Herodotus claims to have seen, seen with his own eyes, if only those portions of it at ground level (not the underground areas), without his having seen fit to specify how they intercommunicated. A building that he was unable to observe or contemplate as a whole, as can readily be done with a Greek temple, and of which he managed to obtain, at best, only views that were myopic, hence partial, fragmentary. Strabo would later describe a labyrinth on a single level, whereas Pliny would multiply its levels, ramps, and stairs. Remaining for the moment with *single-level* labyrinths susceptible to the myopic algorithm discussed above, that of Egypt would indeed qualify, save that we cannot properly speak of its having had *hallways* opening at either end into one or more other hallways (those opening into a single hallway being *dead ends*).[25] The "labyrinth" effect proceeding less from the place's architecture than from the erratic routes it fostered, even in its very symmetry.

Symmetry as a labyrinthine trait? Pierre Rosenstiehl has rightly noted that, in the matter of labyrinths, tortuous paths are useless:

Tortuous windings, local snares, mannered accidents are so many landmarks, and thus are at odds with the project. The architect deploys lines, corners. It is the repetition of motifs that misleads, especially when subtle obliquities, imperceptible and irregular shifts are introduced at the intersections. The "almost regular" confounds the traveler just as it fools the eye of the observer. There can be no question of striving for a chaotic effect by throwing dice to determine the number of hallways leading to a room or the angle of a given passage; for chance—as all experienced gamblers have learned, at their cost—is prodigal with gross accidents that would constitute, in this instance, so many points of orientation in the structure's plan.[26]

If the Egyptian labyrinth eludes the grasp of the logos and its measurement, this is not solely—by contrast with the pyramids— because of its gigantic dimensions and the enormous expense entailed by its construction. If at first, on an initial level, the building seems susceptible to description in terms of constructive mechanics (as in Strabo and, to a still greater degree, in Pliny), our perspective shifts if, in addition, we think of the labyrinth as a ludic space, as the enclosed field of an agonistic game, and as the site of multiple aleatory wanderings, even as a single progress, but one that must obstinately turn back on itself, like interlace. A figure whose line crisscrosses itself to the point of obliterating the ground against which it stands out, but one nonetheless subject to constraints that are not only graphic but also geometric, precisely to the extent that it occupies or covers its assigned field, works it, saturates it. Working this field, saturating it, horizontally, on a single plane, like the only part of the Egyptian labyrinth that Herodotus was allowed to visit, the ground floor, but not to the exclusion of its possible development, in least in imagination, through three dimensions by the addition of floors, an effect amply exploited in Pliny's text. In no way did the entrances to the Egyptian and Cretan labyrinths resemble a descent into Hell. But the Egyptian labyrinth nonetheless featured an inextricable underground dimension whose funerary connotations are obvious (here one thinks of the late medieval prints in which games of chess unfold simultaneously on two levels, that of the living and that of the dead).

How much complexity, how many hallways and intersections, how many "tangles" does it take before a labyrinth begins to be a labyrinth? This is the paradox we evoked in Chapter 1 with regard to piles of sand as well as cities: "How many houses or streets does it take before a town begins to be a town?"[27] Wittgenstein posed this question in conjunction with an analogous one regarding language and what he called its "suburbs." For language, despite its being worthy of the name from its crudest and most primitive man-ifestations, has not always had the extension, the structure, and, above all, the diversity and heterogeneity that now characterize it. It is like the "ancient cities" that Descartes says "have gradually grown from mere villages into large towns." How many houses or streets does it take before a city begins to be a city? How many suburbs, shopping centers, and, within the limits of the same cities, gaps and breaches, redevelopments and additions of all kinds, can there be before an agglomeration loses its urban character? Like cities, lan-guage is never finished, never complete. Was it so, asks Wittgen-stein, before it had absorbed chemical symbols and the notation of the infinitesimal calculus, which imply a concerted linguistic de-velopment (as opposed to its so-called natural developments), and which the author of the *Philosophical Investigations* audaciously likens to "the suburbs of our language"? He goes so far as to compare lan-guage to an old city:

A maze of little streets and squares, of old and new houses, and of houses with additions from various periods; and this surrounded by a multitude of new boroughs with straight regular streets and uniform houses.[28]

The idea of a "pure" labyrinth implies a configuration that is perfectly homogenous and isotropic, one whose circularity and self-sufficiency preclude all manner of extension, and certainly accretions that in any way resemble "suburbs."[29] Yet, as described by Strabo, the Egyptian labyrinth consists of two distinct zones: on the interior (I do not say in the center, labyrinths being acentric by definition[30]), a strictly ordered ensemble of courts surrounded by columns; on the perimeter (the only portion of the complex consistent with the gen-eral understanding of a labyrinth), crypts whose winding passages baffled access to the interior. Paradoxically (keeping to the metaphor of the city and its expansion from an old core, designated "historic," and supposedly the product of a "natural" history, as opposed to later, more studied peripheral developments), order and symmetry seem to have reigned within the building, whereas disorder prevailed on the periphery. But Pierre Rosenstiehl has taught us that labyrinths, however cunning, however closely related to curves plotted on a graph, need not be curvilinear. The "labyrinthine" part of the Egyptian labyrinth was not necessarily where one would have expected it to be. In effect, no hallways and intersections were needed to foil the visitor: if the edifice went beyond the limits of language, if it exceeded anything that could be said about it, this was a matter less of its structure than of the infinite number of possible routes through the complex, which, while undoubtedly immense, was finite. And yet, to cite Wittgenstein again, the metaphor is applicable to language itself, understood as a labyrinth of paths: "You approach from *one* side and know your way about; you approach the same place from another side and no longer know your way about."[31]

"Labyrinth," the word is itself an intersection, like all those constituting thought, words that can lead in any number of directions, down any number of paths.[32] Doubtless we can determine how a word functions by observing how it is used. But the power of the metaphor, when brought to bear on language itself, is nonetheless linked to that dark truth uttered by Borges and inscribed in the word "labyrinth," which holds that the solution to an enigma is never commensurate with the enigma itself.[33] To cite Wittgenstein again, every philosophical problem amounts to a confession that "I don't know my way about."[34] Doubtless we would like to have at our disposal a global representation of the networks of connections that labyrinths amount to *in plan*. Doubtless clear thinking is difficult to reconcile with a *myopic* form of representation,[35] and with a kind of history reducible to the notation of successive passages through the same hallway or intersection—a history, as it were, *de passage(s)*. But what do we know about the desire that grips philosophy, about the desire that haunts the philosopher as far as the heart of the labyrinth, where and when he "doesn't know his way about"? What do we know about what might constitute, for both philosophy and philosopher, the *site* of desire, and its *moment*? And what do we know about this labyrinth of paths that is desire, foreign as it is to algorithms and resistant to all therapies (given that, with desire as with pain, it is language that teaches us the concept)?[36] What do we know about the relation of thought to the labyrinth? What do we know about philosophy *in the labyrinth*: the labyrinth of desire as well as the labyrinth of words; that of language—from which we cannot escape—or that of writing and its games, which are constantly multiplying?

For a Political Graphology

Graphics has become an object as well as a practice of public interest: through the means it uses to construct and display, on walls or in print, the visual identity, or, more simply, to permit any one of us to find his bearings in the mazes (the labyrinths) of cities, but also in those of public agencies, institutions, and administrations, states, at the limit, political regimes, to make legible or reveal, perhaps unbeknownst to themselves, in other words reluctantly, something of their nature, their personality, their deepest tendencies, their project (or lack of same), not to mention their aesthetic, even their ethics. Which is to say that, at the horizon of the reflections prompted by this object and its related practices, one can vaguely make out the profile of a program for an expanded or generalized graphology. Its concern would no longer be, or not exclusively, the handwriting of the individual, whose character supposedly can be inferred from its idiosyncrasies, but rather that of the social body in its entirety, grasped in all the diversity of its graphic manifestations. Hence the idea, if not the project, of a graphology that might be described as "political," in the sense that we speak of political economy, without giving the term any particular partisan coloration but rather construing it, in a way consistent with its etymology, as designating everything pertaining to the city and its operation or government. It's being understood that this etymology refers implicitly, from the start, both to the Greek idea of the polis, the question of the demos, and, through it, to that of democracy. Which necessitates a preliminary exploration of a few byways. Beginning, as is only proper, with that of writing.

To speak of graphics is, in effect (as indicated by the word's derivation from the Greek *graphein*, "to write"), to refer, first, to those marks apparently specific to writing, namely the very tracing of the characters or, to put it differently, the elements of this writing, whether it's a question of pictograms, ideograms, hieroglyphs, or letters of the alphabet. Now these tracings in turn have their own character, or at least their own distinctive characteristics. If graphology is indeed, as the French dictionary says, the "science of the identity of [different forms of] writing," its investigative domain would extend beyond the framework of individual psychiatry to encompass all of a given society or culture's graphic manifestations, which would thus take on the value of symptoms. Over time, the particularities that give an individual's writing its personal stamp become less prominent than what marks it as belonging to a specific historical period. In the same way, the disparity of signs, the absence of a dominant taste in graphics, what might be called the graphic pollution that is characteristic of today's cities, especially those in France, will one day be perceived, in a turn both paradoxical and absurd, as a period trait.

But the very word *line* (which I use here by design), this word, as Roland Barthes points out at the beginning of *Empire of Signs*, has a double connotation, both graphic and linguistic.[1] If the idea of graphics is effectively inseparable from that of language, that is because both graphics and language sustain a relation with writing that might be called originary, or at least foundational, constitutive. Littré, who didn't go that far, defined "*graphisme*" reductively as a "way of representing or writing the words of a language" ("manière de représenter, d'écrire les mots d'une langue"). Nonetheless, the very notion that language might lend itself to something like graphic representation implies, in turn, that anything figurable in drawing, if not images themselves, is somehow caught in language's orbit or field of attraction, whereas language, and a fortiori writing, has an inalienable iconic dimension.

But there is more, and it pertains to graphics [*graphisme*] as conceptualized in its originary, foundational, constitutive relation to writing. For *calligraphy*, defined as the art of properly forming the characters of writing, or as a form of writing subject to the rules of this art, raises, again by way of etymology, the question, if not of beauty, then at least of a specifically aesthetic dimension inhering in graphics per se. What becomes of this question, what befalls this dimension, when we pass from writing traced by hand to *scriptura artificialis*, to mechanical writing, and first of all to print? It is not to be excluded, quite the contrary, that printed characters can have their own beauty, having been designed and shaped in conformity with the rules of art; to such a degree, as Valéry remarked, that an author looking at himself in the mirror of print experiences his own writing differently.[2] Even so, here we should speak not of calligraphy but of typography: technique or symbolics prevailing, by way of "type," over the aesthetic, the *kallos*. As though, while etymology by no means implies this, the beauty of an example of handwriting should definitively be measured in accordance with how much it reveals of the work of the hand, and necessarily the hand of an individual, if not of an artist, of someone who in principle could be designated by name: which brings us back to graphology, narrowly defined.

Thus the projected "political graphology" would encompass that of grammatology as understood by Derrida: a grammatology, a science of writing, concerned not only with possible differences, from the point of view of the "graphic signifier," between various kinds of writing—pictographic, ideographic, hieroglyphic, cuneiform, phonetic, and so forth—potentially in play in graphic communication, but also with that between manuscript and printed text, between manual writing and mechanical writing. Contemporary graphics turns this difference to account and even, I daresay, flaunts it, even as it makes use of every possible resource: sometimes manual writing tries to imitate mechanical writing, in the guise of *script* or by means of stencils, and sometimes mechanical writing attempts a return to its origins, if not with its manual component. Typing, from this perspective, being a kind of compromise, even a regression, toward a mode of graphic communication from which all expressivity has not been erased (the metaphor of the eraser being apt here): according to the *Petit Robert*, the French word for typing, "*dactylographie*," was used around 1900 to designate "the action of expressing oneself by means of touch" (I leave it to the reader to consider, or fantasize about, the meanings and implications of such a definition). Hence, perhaps, the extended vogue in contemporary typography for characters and even page layouts imitating those of typed manuscript. As if to conjure, even on the printed page, something of handwritten script, or at least of the "touch" still crucial to the act of typing, at least until the advent of "digitalized" writing recast the problem. When typography does not renew, purely and simply, with the appealing aspects, sometimes crude and sometimes very sophisticated, of manual writing, with all the risks of infantalization or, conversely, of affectation that might result when the said regression does not answer to a coherent artistic project; such as those, limiting oneself to France, formulated by painters as different as Dubuffet and Adami. The effectiveness of Dutch public graphics being a function of their systematic rejection of any such idea, a posture doubtless influenced by that country's Neoplasticist and reformist traditions.

Even so, the domain now allotted to specialists in "graphics" encompasses much more than strictly linguistic communication. And this is so despite the fact that the idea of writing is inseparable from those, to be concise, of composition and page layout. In the work of today's professional "designers," it is often difficult to distinguish between what pertains to typography, narrowly defined, and what to iconics, the relation between text and image having become a major focus of contemporary graphics. Not to mention the ambition to devise images that might nourish writing and typography—a consequence of the juxtaposition of different kinds of writing that is such an important resource of contemporary graphics. When the image itself does not acquire symbolic force as a logo; which again entails a risk of infantilization, as well as of the rejection of such signature labels, when, for instance, the image in question pictures an animal—a squirrel, say—whose association with saving for the future apparently does not preclude their being captured, and may indeed encourage this [a reference to an advertising campaign for the Caisse d'Épargne, a French savings bank.—Trans.]. And since what is at issue here is money, and the way certain public and private institutions can serve our individual interests, it is worth mentioning a sign that was still visible not too long ago in Burgundy, on Route A6, by way of verbal commentary—in the pedagogic mode that so delights the bureaucrats in charge of French highways—on another, earlier sign picturing buzzards and owls:

USEFUL PREDATORS

We might do well to consider—given that such nonsense corresponds rather well to the countless traps set by graphics supposedly in the public interest—what this sign would mean if, instead of being situated on an open stretch of road, far from an exit, it were placed a few hundred feet from the large toll station at Villefranche-sur-Saône, just before (or after) another sign reading:

PREPARE YOUR CHANGE

We all have our own stories about when it was that we first became aware of the power of state graphics, in circumstances that definitively shaped our ideas about them. In my case, this moment occurred during the occupation, when lists of hostages were posted on walls under the swastika of the Wehrmacht, at the same time that German signs were being grafted onto French ones. A bitter memory, certainly, but one that cannot fully erase that of the general mobilization posters of September 1939, or of Resistance leaflets, or of the wonderful small handbills dropped from allied planes that adolescents such as myself eagerly sought out in the woods around Paris. But even before this period, and indiscriminately with regard to news, propaganda, and intimidation, graphic communication was inscribed within a larger network, linked and even preceded as it was by radio, as it is today by television, in which all of the resources of seeing, reading, and hearing are combined, as had previously been achieved in movies, but with a delay not in play on the "small screen." Proclamation, oral or written, was the form long used by the powers-that-be when they wished to address their subjects, but now there is heated competition among various forms of communication. And as early as 1939, there was a question as to the status and function of notices that had been written, printed, and posted on this sunny September afternoon regarding a mobilization that had been announced on the airwaves at noon. As if such a double and successive inscription, first oral, then written, were necessary to impress the declaration of war on the eye and mind before it could take on the full force of reality.

Happily, the conditions that today shape "public" graphics are less dramatic, but they are also more bureaucratic. It has been said many times before: graphic design figures prominently in all those documents—driver's licenses, passports, credit cards—that now serve to identify us. And it also figures in the morass of red tape—social security cards, notarized papers, tax filings, administrative questionnaires of all kinds—that now documents our passage through this world in the terms and forms deemed suitable by the modern state. This state of affairs is only natural, or at least normal. For it is difficult to see how we might dispense with this polyglot jumble, which is both an instrument and a sign of freedom (to become convinced of this, one need only be deprived, even for a very short time, of one's passport or driver's license). But this commonsense observation does not imply that we can afford to ignore the specific graphic means used by the state to administer the social body, quite the contrary. For these means, in addition to conveying information, cannot fail to affect the formation of citizens, beginning with what we will call straight-out their aesthetic formation, and with the development of collective taste.

Many historians and others will have discovered only retrospectively, on seeing such agitprop posters Vladimir Mayakovsky's "windows" for the Soviet telegraph office (ROSTA) and John Heartfield's photomontages, the potential power of such imagery, whether produced in defense of revolution or in opposition to Nazi grandiloquence. Graphics is not a matter of grandiloquence and does not always sit well with it, although it can yield to its ends, as evidenced by the impact still produced, in both formal and symbolic terms, by the swastika. Fortunately, however, the time is now past when Walter Benjamin felt obliged to counter the totalitarian aestheticization of politics with a "revolutionary" politicization of the aesthetic. It is the luck, the price, the condition of democracy to escape from the rhetoric of chiasmus. To such a point that the only real question now pertinent to public graphics is that of its utility and, to a still greater degree (from the commissioning agency to the professionals it addresses, turning one's back resolutely on both the strategies of advertising and the ideology of communication), that of its deployment, of its democratic application. It has become an affair of ethics as much as of aesthetics.

Tocqueville, not unreasonably, was concerned about the minimal role accorded aesthetic considerations in American democracy. But that is because he still credited traditional notions of art promulgated by the academies. As Stendhal would later say, in more appropriate terms: over there, nothing but shopkeepers; and no opera. Regarding opera, his misjudgment is a matter of record.[3] As to business, and the money that is its instrument and its end, things are not as simple as they might at first seem. Regarding the dollar bill, the "greenback," which now circulates throughout the world as— to use Marx's terminology—the country's most "general" equivalent, it seems clear that at least some of its prestige derives from what must surely be considered its stunning graphic success (format, color, the subtle relationship between recto and verso, the way the design template can accommodate various numerical values and likenesses of America's founding fathers) and from a political will to continuity, even permanence, evidenced as well by America's telling retention over the years of its coins (quarter, dime, nickel, penny).

The swastika has now been relegated to the warehouse, like the hammer and sickle (which—alas!—is not to say that they can't still be put to dark uses). But the symbol of the dollar, this S traversed by a vertical line that many long argued was a capitalist imposition as infamous as the emblems of totalitarianism, this sign, this mark, has not managed to eclipse the image, otherwise more commanding and more allusive, of the dollar bill. General de Gaulle revealed his understanding of the symbolic network within which money operates when he tried, by means of a graphic sleight of hand (the suppression of two zeros), to restore to the franc some of the heft it had lost. It seems fair to say, at the very least, that on this occasion the state's graphics were not adequate to its intentions.

Far from praising the dollar, or defending it, I wish here only to point out that democracy, for better and worse, might have to familiarize itself with the aesthetic. Note my choice of words: *familiarize itself* with it. For there is not, nor can there ever be, a democratic aesthetic. It is certainly not my intention—paraphrasing Benjamin—to oppose an aestheticization of democracy by advocating a democratization of the aesthetic. Rather, the task would be to ponder the conditions under which, if not art in general, then at least the collective arts of architecture, design, and above all public graphics, might be practiced democratically (this being said for the sake of those who continue, against all reason, to insist that there are no political options other than reformism and its denunciation). And to probe the extent to which questions of taste could and should enter into democratic debate, even into the debate about democracy itself, and about the form in which these questions—questions, again, of *taste*—could and should come to constitute a veritable stake for democracy and for its institution, always being renewed, always being reworked, as will be shown by what follows.

4

Made in Germany

West Berlin, May 1978: a city under siege yet open, without apparent walls or defenses, apart from the discreet patrolling of the jeeps of the American Military Police and the BMWs of the federal police. As with any siege, there must be fortifications, or at least a wall, and here this was built not by the besieged but by the besiegers, not so much to surround the other as in self-defense against the fascination exerted by the other, and to prevent defection from within its own ranks. In this sense, the Berlin Wall marked a singular advance in the "de-construction" of the binary oppositions upon which our culture rests: here we are far from Hadrian's Wall, which excluded the hordes of the north and marked the limit of the Roman world; far from the Great Wall of China, as from any notion of a boundary between humanity and barbarism; far from any idea of an apportionment between the two.

A wall: in truth, at least in its most recent form (1967), a mere barrier, a simple partition that now—the moment of riots and tragedy, of the wall of elbow-to-elbow *vopos* (soldiers), of the blockade and the airlift, of would-be escapees being shot on sight having receded into the past—seems absurdly miserable, a construction that the police of the Western sector even had to protect with fences from the onslaughts of political graffiti and obscene inscriptions, the two often being identical: *Honecker = Breichnevs Schuhputzer* ("Honecker = Breshnev's bootblack"); *Dirty needs*; *Wir werden die Mauern mitsprengen* ("We'll blow up the wall"); *Axeman rules all, suck my cock*; *Jimmy Carter wir grüben dich* ("Jimmy Carter, we buried you"). "Modernity" (the wall already belongs to the history of architecture, including the sheets of plastic spread over parts of it—*yellow* plastic: *Start Jagd auf Juden* ["Jew-hunt starts here"]) having failed to extend its grip over the entirety of the frontier, the wall was hastily thrown together, the besiegers-besieged having had to defend themselves against attacks other than the draining away or desperate charges of their own dissidents. On Bernauer Strasse, the facades of buildings emptied of their occupants were simply smoothed over, all their apertures walled-up (remember the waterfront at Mers-les-Bains in 1946, opposite Tréport, with its half-timber gables overwhelmed by concrete fortifications "made in France" for the German Todt organization).

When I went to see it for the first time in June 1978, near the old Reichstag, workers were busy shifting it forward a few feet, as if to give wide berth to this blaze of writing. A crane replaced one after another of the prefabricated concrete panels that the soldiers then whitewashed after capping them with a kind of drainpipe, while a cordon of *vopos* kept guard in front of the provisional breach created by the operation. One of them, a low-ranking officer equipped with binoculars and a camera with a huge magnifying lens, systematically photographed the license plates of the cars of foreign tourists who had come to witness the spectacle, a story of *seeing*, of looking *from the other side*, from the vantage of wooden observation platforms built expressly for the purpose opposite the observation posts in the eastern sector. Some days later, we would pass—without a hitch, although not without a number of formalities and a thorough search —through the only access point open to private cars: Checkpoint Charlie.

Near the Brandenburg Gate, where during the riots of June 1953 protesters had ripped town the red flag atop the quadriga (before the eyes of Soviet soldiers, soon to be replaced by barricades), the wall gave way to a stockade that made it possible to see, through Langhans's propylaeum, the perspective down the Lindenstrasse. In front of a handrail where the people of the West came to lean, this sign having been posted for their information: "Achtung. Sie verlassen jetzt Berlin-West" ("Attention. You are now leaving West Berlin"). And there, beyond a parterre of flowers and the people opposite who looked at us, the only eye-level breach in the wall (I remember the "no-man's-land" north of Central Park, before the entry into Harlem, five or six deserted streets, traversed by no gazes, like a white person venturing beyond 125th Street: in 1963, during Kennedy's visit to Berlin, large red curtains were hung between the columns of the Brandenburg Gate to block the perspective and block the exchange of gazes). One could just make out in the distance Karl Friedrich Schinkel's Neue Wache, transformed into a memorial to the victims of fascism and militarism [*sic*], in front of which goose-step changes of the guard took place every morning.

We were surprised, once past the wall (regularly whitewashed, most recently for the visit of President Carter), having entered the gray world of the East and made our way onto a fog-gripped Museum Island to visit the Pergamon Museum, having walked down the Babylonian processional causeway and through the gate of Ishtar (the tension of the color, the Orient—the East is *gray*—being blue and gold), reconstructed such that the market gate from Miletus is fixed to its back; we were surprised to discover, at the end of this walled progression, that fragments of the gigantomachy formerly installed around the Pergamon altar (I suddenly remember, again, before that of Miletus in stormy weather, the vision of the simple cube of earth still extant in Pergamon among the pines, seen in a plunging view from the acropolis, flooded by southern light); yes, we were surprised to discover that the exterior frieze had been installed—like that of the Parthenon in the British Museum—against the room's walls to either side of the altar facade, the monument having been turned inside out like a glove, the museum having dismantled its exterior, and that the said frieze was arrayed against a wall made of slabs of the same type and almost the same dimensions as those used to build the "wall of shame."

Recto/verso, obverse/reverse: the wall—like an *écorché*, like a ruin: the ruin that it was from the beginning—had no readily identifiable wrong side. As for the decor that accumulated over it, that sullied it, this furious scriptomachy was never anything other than a spectacle staged by the West, among the many souvenir and post-card shops, for itself, and of which the people on the other side, like the prisoners in Plato's cave, perceived only an echo (in the distance, beyond the no-man's-land scattered with chevaux-de-frise on the site formerly occupied by the Potsdamer Platz, the tower of East German television, the Fernsehturm, a concrete column 820 feet high that, according to the *Guide Bleu*, offered an "impregnable" view of Berlin—the manifesto of another modernity, the same one?). The "German soul" (in front of the wall we were all "German Jews") exhibiting on a screen behind which its double was contained, and for the exclusive use and instruction of Western tourists and important visitors, its obverseless surface. One inscription among others, at the opening, marked by a stake, of what once had been Potsdamer Strasse: "Made in Germany."

5

A Very Special Museum

In one of his most famous novellas, as well as one of his most
beautiful and singular, Jorge Luis Borges recounts the story—the
fable, rather—of the "Immortals" who, weary of the condition to
which they had been reduced by drinking water from the stream
that "purifies men of death," ended by destroying the resplendent
city in which they lived and infesting caves along the same stream,
where they proceeded to live like Troglodytes, abdicating "verbal
commerce" and surviving on a diet of snakes.

Thus far the fable has a consoling effect, at least by antithesis,
for readers know themselves to be mortal. As the narrator says,
"What is divine, terrible, and incomprehensible is *to know* oneself
immortal." Immortality effectively drains away meaning: given infinite time, everything must of necessity happen to everyone, from
which it follows that no one has an individual existence, and that
good and evil, genius and idiocy, indeed all human endeavors can-
cel one another out in "a system of exact compensations." Things
grow more complicated, however, when, after having destroyed the
City whose renown had spread far and wide, the Immortals deem
it good to build, on the same site, using its ruins, a second City, a
kind of "parody or antithesis" of the first one—so the narrator tells

us—that was also a temple to the irrational gods who govern the world and "about whom we know nothing save that they do not resemble man." A City unknown to antiquity, predating humanity, predating—if this is possible—the earth itself, a construction that, in the eyes of the visitor, is associated with atrocity, with complete nonsense:

I had made my way through a dark maze, but it was the bright City of the Immortals that terrified and repelled me. A maze is a house built purposely to confuse men; its architecture, prodigal in symmetries, is made to serve that purpose. In the palace that I imperfectly explored, the architecture had *no* purpose. There were corridors that led nowhere, unreachably high windows, grandly dramatic doors that opened onto monklike cells or empty shafts, incredible upside-down staircases with upside-down treads and balustrades. Other staircases, clinging airily to the side of a monumental wall, petered out after two or three landings, in the high gloom of the cupolas, arriving nowhere. . . . *This City*, I thought, *is so horrific that its mere existence, the mere fact of its having endured—even in the middle of a secret desert—pollutes the past and the future and somehow compromises the stars. So long as this City endures, no one in the world can ever be happy or courageous.*[1]

The idea of building this second City was the idea of an Immortal named Homer. And that, we are told, should not surprise us: "It is rumored that after singing the war of Ilion, he sang of the war between the frogs and rats. He was like a god who created first the Cosmos, then Chaos." This, according to the fable, was the last *symbol* to which the Immortals condescended: "It marks the point at which, esteeming all exertion vain, they resolved to live in thought, in pure speculation."

Rich as it was in "bulwarks and amphitheaters and temples," did the City of the Immortals have a museum? The question might seem idle: Of what interest, utility, or consolation would such an institution have been to the Immortals, seeing as it could only have confirmed for them the idea of the purely aleatory and contingent character of the works of men pretending in one way or another to immortality? ("Homer composed the *Odyssey*; given infinite time, with infinite circumstances and changes, it is impossible that the *Odyssey* should *not* be composed at least once.") But temples? Amphitheaters? What cults, what spectacles, what speeches could have led the Immortals to assemble in them and discuss their own nothingness? And if we posit that the city itself had assumed the character of a museum, as is too often the case for our cities, for us mortals, we can see how paradoxical is the notion of a city sharing in the immortal condition of its inhabitants: a city that is itself indestructible, even its lesser buildings, the most insignificant of its structures, in a way analogous to—according to Freud—the indiscriminately retentive character of unconscious memory. We can understand how the Immortals would have wanted to rid themselves of this nightmare: a nightmare all too manifestly related to what Françoise Choay has called "the allegory of patrimony"[2]; related to the idea of the "monument"; related to the idea of the "museum"; but related, also, to the very idea of "architecture," and all its attendant presuppositions, all the images and metaphors that follow from it (about which Georges Bataille was the first to note the degree to which they can infect thought), all the oppositional plays that we now strive to "deconstruct." For like it or not, the word is linked, is related, to the idea of *arché*—to that of beginning, of principle, of foundation, as well as to that of structure: architectonics, said Kant, is the art of systems.

A nightmare, then, from which it was impossible for the Immortals to awaken, and from which they could escape only by falling into an archaic torpor. This makes it all the more remarkable that they reached that stage by way of a final "foundation"—"*fundación*" is the term Borges gives his narrator—that must have functioned as a symbol, and as such have been laden with meaning, but a meaning inscribed, as that of symbols should be, in its form, in its very architecture, however arbitrary and incongruous the latter might seem. As though, in order to extract themselves from the nightmare of an interminable history and attain a parodic absolute knowledge in which the mind is in direct contact with itself, without need of resorting to intermediate sensations or signs, they had to seek shelter in caves, thereby regressing to a stage prior to all architecture, all the while remaining—without penetrating it, knowing nothing of it, having forgotten it—in close proximity to this improbable City in which all means, all techniques, all science, but also all forms, all elements, all motifs that might pertain to the art of building had been used, the better to deny and abuse, in symbolic terms, the values regarded as inherent in the very term "architecture": the same architecture that Hegel regarded as the first of all the arts as well as the "symbolic" art par excellence.[3]

For such was indeed the function of the buildings that the narrator explored after having himself drunk from the impure stream (the description now detailing not avenues, temples, or amphitheaters but a palace): to bring up short, by means of their merciless permanence, any fantasy the Immortals might have had of introducing into the duration without beginning or end that was their lot (duration, not eternity) some semblance of history, or at least of narrative, as well as of the idea of building, of construction, but also of conservation—in a word: of permanence. Which brings us, again by antithesis, to the question of the museum, and specifically to that of the museum of architecture, which takes on a singular relief in this light. For if humanity has always sustained fantasies inverse to those of the Immortals, dreaming of conferring on history, primarily by means of architecture, a dimension that is, if not eternal, then at least durable, the institution of the museum cannot fail to have renewed this fantasy, its first effect being to bring to an end—at least as regards the art of building—the cult of ruins, to initiate another way of relating to antiquity, one that, instead of being picturesque and nostalgic, is constructive and explicitly oriented toward the future.

Werner Szambien has recounted in magisterial fashion the history—not brilliant, in truth, but nonetheless exemplary—of the idea of a museum of architecture such as this was formulated for the first time in France, on the eve of the Terror.[4] Should we be surprised by this? The Revolution, through the mouthpiece of Étienne-Louis Boullée, among others, put the question of the museum of architecture on the agenda, the idea being not to institute a place that would welcome the more or less utopian projects for monuments and buildings dreamed up by the "revolutionary" architects (beginning with Boullée himself) in a manner consistent with the new order of things, but rather to present, in the best possible conditions, an ensemble of objects and models likely to nourish and enflame the imagination of artists and patrons as well as that of the "architecture-loving" public, which was still quite small. In this context, it is worth noting, following Szambien, that—contrary to current fashion—what is often called (somewhat glibly) "paper architecture," purely graphic designs, restricted to the two-dimensional plane, originally figured not at all in the constitution of the museum of architecture, which was open to the most varied techniques of representation and reproduction, with one signal exception: drawing.[5]

The history of the museum of architecture is exemplary in more than one respect, above all because it poses with maximum clarity a set of questions likewise occasioned by the present revival of this idea, support for which now—at a moment when the word "terror" has lost all of its revolutionary connotations—seems to be unanimous. This unanimity (or its appearance) is of course suspicious, given the variety of interests in play and, still more, the diversity of the designs accruing authority from the idea, which often differ radically among themselves. A museum of what, composed how, for whom, and to what end(s)? One's answers to these questions will of course be anything but innocent. And it is not by chance that the initial formulation of these questions and answers coincided with the moment of definitive rupture with the Old Regime, when there was widespread belief, for the first time, in the double possibility of building a new world and doing so with means that were, preeminently, those of architecture. Things are very different now, when not only the notion of the museum is in question but also those of architecture and construction, as well as—it bears repeating—all the values potentially accruing to them. With the caveat that, today as yesterday, at a distance of two centuries, the history from which the constructivists thought they could free themselves is again bearing down with all its blind weight. The history, but no longer the utopia, whose sole refuge for the moment is science fiction.

In its initial form, and in a way that might indeed be called (as we shall see) revolutionary, the museum of architecture—described at the time as "special"—answered a specific need and addressed a specific public, even as it brought together objects of a specific kind. Doubtless architecture merited a place in the Louvre, among the arts of drawing in what would become, in 1793, the Musée Central des Arts. In light of this expectation, the depot at the Petits-Augustins, the core of Alexandre Lenoir's future Musée des Monuments Français, provisionally housed architectural fragments appropriated from the property of the church, émigrés, and finally from those of the crown, to guarantee their safety and make sure that they would be "placed at the disposition of the nation," save for those that might serve to embellish extant buildings. As Françoise Choay has noted, we are very conscious of the havoc wrought by revolutionary vandals, but the Revolution's project to safeguard what was then coming to be known as the French patrimony remains largely unknown. Heritage, succession, patrimony, conservation: from the beginning, the authorities adopted the metaphor of succession to designate and administer this treasure.[6] But the intention to transform the Louvre, the most symbolic of all French sites, into the prime receptacle for the nation's artistic riches demonstrates nicely how rupture with the Old Regime went hand-in-hand with an affirmation of continuity that was effectively patrimonial, and preeminently real-estate oriented. In this sense, constituted as it was by pieces of architecture and sculpture "wrested from the hands of destruction," the museum of Alexandre Lenoir was consistent with one of the functions it is tempting to ascribe to a museum of architecture, namely the advancement of historical preservation and historical pedagogy, goals held to be at least equal in importance to that of civic education. As Michelet noted, it was here that the young Romantics discovered "the true order of eras" as well as "the absolute relativity of every age and style"[7]—which is why, as Anthony Vidler has suggested, Quatremère de Quincy fought so relentlessly for its closure.

Specialists and art professionals advocated a very different kind of museum. They did not, I repeat, imagine it as a receptacle for projects and dreams, for the full gamut of fantasies to which architects were prone (but which were in fact not the least bit "fantastic"), confined largely to paper. Submissions to the design competition for a projected museum of architecture (or if you prefer, of revolutionary architecture) organized in the Year II—apparently the first architectural competition conceived along lines that have since become familiar to us—had to be rather fully worked out: the rules stipulated that the winning designs be reproduced as maquettes and carefully preserved, so as to constitute over time "a collection of models."[8] This notion of the "model" was basic to the project for a "musée spéciale d'architecture," but in ways that were by no means specifically contemporary.

Werner Szambien has shown that the project for a museum of architecture, in process during the Terror, was a characteristic product of the second half of the eighteenth century, and that it was an extension of endeavors then thought to be as much archaeological as architectural, for example *Les Ruines des plus beaux monuments de la Grèce considérées du côté de l'Histoire et de l'Architecture* by Julien-David Le Roy (1758) and Gabriel-Pierre-Martin Dumont's presentation of Soufflot's discovery of the ruins of Paestum.[9] The publication of the first "visual" travel accounts, a genre conceived by the English, who illustrated them lavishly, was viewed as a public good, a utilitarian project that reached its culmination and its end simultaneously in the Egyptian expedition. But however interesting, allusive, and seductive—in a word, picturesque—the images in the *Description de l'Égypte*, however precise and objective their renderings of ancient buildings, these volumes were nonetheless marred by a striving for effect, especially in their handling of perspective, that their many plans, sections, and elevations did not suffice to correct. By comparison with these illustrations, which are often approximate (as Champollion suspected, to the ire of the authorities responsible for the Egyptian expedition), the plaster casts made directly from architectural and ornamental motifs—another novelty—held every promise of being precise, whereas the models—of recent invention,

realized in three dimensions in cork or other materials and to scale
—created an entirely different effect, making it possible to take in a
building at a glance.[10] But above all, these models, like the plaster
casts, were less representations than reproductions, and thus facilitated reconstitutions that, breaking with the taste for, the cult and
ideology of the ruin, were of such technical perfection that they imposed themselves as "models" in their own right, to such an extent
that they were able to enflame and—as was already being said—
"electrify" the imagination.[11]

I will not dwell here on the acknowledged value of Greek and
Roman models under the Terror, until those of Egypt were added
under the Empire, simultaneous with the emergence, in reaction
against the vandalism surreptitiously encouraged by the successive
early Revolutionary governments, of a new sensitivity regarding
the national patrimony, beginning with the Gothic, so long deni-
grated.[12] Marx wrote astutely about the pervasive feeling among
contemporary men that donning antique masks would make it easier for them to confront the tasks assigned them by history. What
matters here is that the initial emergence of the idea of a museum
of architecture coincided precisely with a moment in which, as regards the art of building, the level of reproduction might have
seemed, a good half-century before the invention of photography,
to interfere with that of representation, even to short-circuit it. And
yet, while it is accurate to say, as does Werner Szambien, that the
production of models constituted an implicit critique of the means
of representation current in the period[13] (beginning with strictly
graphic ones), it does not follow from this that the museum of architecture escaped from the circuit of representation. Assuming
that cities themselves are not deemed the only viable museums of
architecture, such institutions differ in principle from other museums, for example those of painting and sculpture, in that they cannot accommodate actual works of art, save very occasionally (as
with the Temple of Dendur, now in the Metropolitan Museum of
Art, New York) or in the form of fragments taken directly from
buildings or cast in plaster—or in the form of simulacra, which is

precisely what scale models are. The mere fact that the administrators were, in principle and to the extent their resources allowed, completely free to commission models of whatever monuments and buildings they deemed appropriate, set the museum of architecture apart from other types of public collection, its brief being not so much to conserve artifacts as to educate a specialized public; a distinction that eventually led to its demise. In the field of architecture, not only was the "real" museum preceded by the imaginary one, historically as well as in the guise of the varied publications in which imaged representations played the largest role, the former—as an institution, as a site of memory, at the limit, even in its built form—was inscribed within an imaginary and conceptual field far exceeding the limits of the collections it housed. Doubtless this holds, to some extent, for every museum. But the kind of memories and cultural associations that can so enrich our experience of museums of painting and sculpture would have been, at least initially, utterly crucial to the functioning, in both historical and comparative terms, of the museum of architecture, its having been premised, from the start, on the technical reproducibility of architectural productions, the imaginary component necessarily prevailing in it over all others.

What does this have to do with Borges's Immortals and the parody of the city that they felt compelled to build to indicate their refusal of their condition? At the moment of its initial institution, during the Terror, history and memory were very much implicated in the museum of architecture, as was the overthrow of an established order that accommodated only too well the renewed affirmation of the perpetuity of classical models and the continuity of a cherished inheritance. Save, I repeat, that, as regards architecture, the functions of conservation and edification (in the pedagogic sense of the word) would initially have been strictly dissociated. The Revolution, at the same time that it inscribed on its agenda the creation of a museum of architectural *models*, introduced—the two functions being explicitly separated—the notion of "monuments" declared to be "historic," which is to say monuments that could not, by their very nature, be stored away but that nonetheless seemed worth preserving in more than image. It is but a short step from this notion to conceiving of the city itself as a museum, and a museum, preeminently, of architecture, one that would have nothing imaginary about it because the monuments themselves would be preserved there, in situ, with or without the adjacent urban tissue. But it is clear that such a notion would put into question not only the idea of the museum and the idea of the city but also that of architecture itself, insofar as it is a project oriented by definition toward the future.

Contemporary tourists who go to Rome, as pilgrims did in the past, do not fail, time permitting, to visit, near Tivoli, in the immediate environs of the city itself said to be "eternal," a spectacular set of ruins known as Hadrian's Villa. Doubtless this immense architectural complex, built by the Emperor Hadrian, that great dilettante, at the end of his life as a kind of final refuge, did not in the slightest resemble an inside-out city. Yet occasionally, when walking there, I have thought about Borges's troglodytes, if only because of the manifestly ludic, even parodic, character of many of the structures scattered among the site's trees, valleys, and hills. Not to mention how, although some of the buildings with domes whose structures are relatively well preserved seem anachronistic, and although the functions of these varied constructions, which include a "maritime theater" and a large arcaded esplanade, are not always clear, there can be no question as to the site's general character as a "theater of memory." But here again, it is important to avoid being seduced by words, or rather by names. Although several of these buildings house replicas of famous works of art, fine ancient copies of classical statuary, including replicas of the Erechtheion caryatids, found in the "Canopus," as well as mosaic floors emulating the Hellenistic practice of reproducing famous paintings, we must not allow ourselves to be deceived by the names given to these structures (beginning with "Canopus," evocative of ancient Egypt): contrary to a glib notion that is widespread, these buildings were not intended to reproduce those that the emperor had visited in the course of his travels, although the names attached to them might indeed have prompted such memories in him.[14]

Françoise Choay has nonetheless described Hadrian's Villa as "the first museum of architecture at actual scale."[15] But a museum in what sense, if tourists are not permitted to visit buildings deemed too fragile, in accordance with the practice of many open-air museums in Scandinavia and the United States, especially as regards wooden structures? And if there are no full-scale reproductions of buildings analogous to those of statues and paintings, such as were to be found in Pergamon under the Attalids (given to erecting copies of large Hellenistic monuments in their capital), or like the life-size reproduction of the Parthenon now in Nashville, Tennessee. As though, in the matter of architecture, fact counted less, in its museum, than idea, history less than utopia, the real less than the imaginary or the symbolic. It has been suggested that Hadrian's Villa is a kind of architectural treatise written in stone, in bricks and mortar as well as in light and shadow, in water, earth, and vegetation. Piranesi already saw it in much this way: not in terms of parody, but as a kind of paradigmatic, if irreparably ruined, free variation on the basics of ancient architecture, which found here, and in the palace of Diocletian in Split, their ultimate expression, in large part fantasmatic.

Should we be surprised that, among contemporary museums of architecture, one of the first to be built expressly for this purpose, the one recently erected in Frankfurt to designs by Oswald Mathias Ungers, is organized in large part around what its author calls its "thematic component," its fictional dimension:[16] the building having been conceived not only to house the German museum of architecture but also to represent, to signify, in its appearance, in its very disposition such as this reveals itself to visitors, what architecture is and could be? That this museum should be situated inside a large villa built early in the present century, and whose architecture, however crudely, sought to evoke that of Michelangelo's Laurentian Library: such a choice assumes particular significance in the context of a city that has suffered destruction on so massive a scale. But what matters still more is that, in the center of this house, Ungers erected another one that rises clear through it, from top to bottom: an empty structure in the form of a tower, rectangular in plan, that can be described as minimalist and archetypal, given that it rests on four pillars that evoke a baldachin (a structural type in which John Summerson has seen the origin of architecture), and around which are distributed, on four levels, exhibition rooms that, on the occasion of the opening, housed a show devoted to the many new museums in Frankfurt. As if this nested configuration were meant to imply that architecture and the museum are indissociable. To phrase this differently: as if, the validity of the idea of a museum of architecture having been assumed, the institution were obliged to compensate, by the means of architecture but in the mode of fiction, for the constitutive lack specific to the art of building, or, if you prefer, for its essential void, as manifested in the fable of the upside-down city, turned inside out like a glove, erected by the Immortals. The same lack, the same void that Hegel tries to conjure, positing the Tower of Babel as its origin in architecture—a building, according to Herodotus, that was not hollow inside but solid, with thick walls, a *purgos stereos*.[17]

The link thus created between architecture and the museum has a double meaning: while the institution is capable of restoring to the art of building some of the symbolic value that it has lost by the importance increasingly accorded use value or function, it expects of architecture in return not only that it procure for it the spaces it needs, but also that it strengthen the museum's desired self-image. At a moment when the museum has demonstrated its ability to receive, control, and even organize the contestation of which it is supposedly the object, and with it all the values it is charged with defending, beginning with that of "art," we have reason to interrogate it about the deep reasons that might have prompted it to open its doors to architecture, a domain that had hitherto eluded its grasp. In this regard, and remaining in the realm of symbols, it was not by chance that the part of the Centre Georges Pompidou originally dubbed the "forum"—a misleadingly grandiloquent name—should have been transformed into an exhibition space at the very moment when a show advocating a particular notion of what a museum of architecture should be opened on the fifth floor (see below). Conversely, the fact of the art of building's finding itself within an institution, as a museological object, inevitably raises questions about the very concept of architecture and the uses (Georges Bataille would say: the *besognes*, or "needs") of the word—a "crossroads" word if ever there was one—as well about the *artifact* that it designates, about the ends that might be assigned to architecture, about the conditions and forms of its practice, about its proper place, and at the same time about the place that the museum constitutes, institutes, represents for it, including in its own architecture.

A place, in this instance, that is not only, that is not initially, a place of exhibition: architecture has its own particular way of presenting itself to vision, of *exhibiting* itself; and it would be an abdication if it were to turn to the museum to program its own reception or—worse still—to achieve one form or another of legitimation. But a place, likewise, that is neither exclusively nor initially a site of memory. Although it can shelter a few fragments, the preeminent function of the museum of architecture is not the preservation of monuments, nor even of their images, save in the derivative—I do not say substitutive—form of models and graphic representations. In the end, even a full-scale museum of architecture such as Hadrian's Villa might be presents the visitor not so much with examples as with a kind of paradigm of what ancient architecture might have been: and "paradigm," as Derrida has noted, is another of those words related to architecture, and in two senses, insofar as *paradeigma* designates, for example (an example of something that is itself exemplary), "an architect's plan," and that the paradigm, the model of conjugation and declension proposed by architecture, can figure, metaphorically and otherwise, in fields other than that of physical construction, as when we speak, for example, of the architecture of a language or of any system whatever.[18] My thesis, which is by no means original and which corresponds quite closely to the one advanced by the Centre Georges Pompidou in its 1991 exhibition "Manifeste," is that the museum of architecture should accommodate only objects that might serve as examples or models, but in the strictly theoretical, epistemological, projective, or, even better, projectile sense of these terms (*"projectile"* designating, according to Littré, that which flings, hurls, or throws; that which produces a projection or inference of some kind). What the public, the general public as well as the specialized public, wants from a museum, in the matter of architecture, is not so much models that lend themselves to imitation, or agreeable images, representations intended to seduce, as information bearing upon what is, or what could be, the process of design-work: which inevitably entails criticism of the current practice of architecture, and of the institutional, ideological, and political factors that shape it.

Design-work is the focus of many objects and images already in traditional museums and collections, specialized and otherwise, whether the Museo dell'Opera in Florence, which houses the wooden model of Brunelleschi's dome, or the analogous museum in Strasbourg, which owns drawings for parts of the facade and towers of the cathedral, and also museums of painting, drawing cabinets, and collections like those of the king of Sweden and the Royal Institute of Architects in London, to say nothing of the collection of the Académie d'Architecture recently shown at the Pavillon de l'Arsenal. An exhibition mounted at Palazzo Grassi in Venice, in 1994, included a number of models and paintings, many of them justly celebrated, relating to the development of Italian Renaissance architecture.[19] The fact that one encountered there Brunelleschi's above-mentioned model for the dome of Florence cathedral and Michelangelo's model for the facade of San Lorenzo, as well as one of the three perspective views known as *urbinates* that have long fascinated me,[20] suffices to demonstrate the breadth of the field to which we refer when we speak of architectural "design" or architectural "models" (for the above-mentioned perspective paintings are indeed "models," despite their being confined to two dimensions). Not to mention that, where architecture is concerned, design-work need not entail the production of models, or even that of drawings. To those astonished by the survival of so very few graphic documents relating to medieval architecture, I would point out that, although there must have been resort to models of some kind, buildings themselves, or specific parts of them, could have served this purpose, and the same holds for ancient architecture as for that of the Romanesque and Gothic periods.[21] This being said by way of evoking, in passing, everything that, by definition, would elude the grasp of the museum, however "special" it might aim to be, or be said to be.

The Palazzo Grassi exhibition itself functioned as a kind of model, alas short-lived, of what a museum of Italian Renaissance architecture might be. But even if we bracket out the museum's function of preservation, it still would not be reduced to a site of memory, much less an archival depository, for of necessity it would have to engage two notions simultaneously, that of the museum and that of architecture. If there is to be a museum of architecture, its function should be preeminently pedagogical, as was the intention of its supporters in the period of the Terror. But it should also accommodate critical and even philosophical perspectives, rather like the upside-down city conceived by Borges's Immortals and near which they decided to remain. Which amounts to saying that there can be no museum of architecture, in the "veritable" ["*véridique*"] —as opposed to the "true" ["*vraie*"]—sense of the words "museum" and "architecture," unless it is strictly contemporary and directly linked to current architectural practice.

The idea of establishing a gallery of modern architecture was born at the Museum of Modern Art in New York, with two exhibitions mounted a quarter-century apart. The first one, organized by Philip Johnson and Henry-Russell Hitchcock, presented the American public with its first image of what was already known as the "international style," calling upon American architects to situate themselves within it.[22] The second one, which opened in New York in 1959, after the great wave of emigration had brought many masters of the modern movement to the United States, was devoted to an institution that seemed to best sum up their enterprise: the Bauhaus.[23] Profiting from their expertise and experience, Alfred Barr and his successors, much aided by Philip Johnson, managed to assemble what might be described as a collection linked to modern architecture, one including several original models and many drawings, including a very large group by Mies Van der Rohe. But it also included models realized after the fact, which is to say reduced-scale models of several key buildings of the modern movement. Thereby affirming the pedagogical role that might be performed by a museum of *modern* art.

It is perhaps useful to recall here that it was within the field of architecture that a critique of modernity first developed. As was only natural, given architecture's key role in defining this same modernity, and in its material production as well as its imaginary projection, as was demonstrated early on, to striking effect, by the Museum of Modern Art's Bauhaus exhibition. The will to escape from the ideological and institutional system within which architects were the first to be enclosed; the concern to signal a moment of hiatus, in other words to institute a kind of architectural moratorium; and, above all, the aim of restoring to architecture some of the semantic energy stripped from it by the adherents of "functionalism": all of these factors prompted many architects to devote themselves to what has been called "paper architecture," with drawing assuming all functions inscribable under the heading "representation." The exhibition organized by the Centre Pompidou in 1984, under the title "Images et imaginaires d'architecture," set the tone, calling for the establishment of an international museum of modern architecture. This exhibition consisted exclusively, as regards architecture, of images thought to awaken or rekindle desire, while pretending to help reconstitute a common language, one capable of accommodating genuine critical debate. At roughly the same time, several galleries opened in New York and elsewhere in hopes of exploiting this lode, as had already been done with photography and, as early as the eighteenth century, with cork models.

The fact that almost ten years later the exhibition "Manifeste," mounted by the Centre Pompidou to assess its own activity, included, in addition to many related drawings, some very beautiful working models by contemporary architects, and that at the same moment a gallery specializing in such objects opened in Paris, evidences an evolution consistent with the tendency I have been describing: that of an interrogation of what design-work—architecture as *work*—is, and what it might be. It is no longer a question merely of describing an opposition between the real practices of architects and a set of imaginary practices, but of understanding, by means of the museum, the nature of the relationship between conception and realization. To put this differently, using, with some hesitation, the language of "deconstruction": of using the museum to raise doubts about the supposed opposition between the art of building and building itself, between architecture and construction. And this, not to confuse the two or to reduce the one to the other, or even to suggest that the silent order of the built is superseded by a rhetorical order specific to architecture, but to improve our understanding of the nature, actual or potential (the latter being a persistent concern), with regard to architecture, of *construction.* As Philippe Boudon noted in the catalogue of the exhibition "Images et imaginaires d'architecture," there is a radical difference between an architectural drawing whose sole function is to communicate or represent, and an architectural drawing that serves to advance the process of elaboration, and whose referent, while part of the developmental process, is nonetheless subject to specifically structural constraints insofar as it is meant to be "realizable."[24] But the museum, by abstracting the objects it receives from their contexts and delivering them from their functions, weaves between them new relations, ones that have the advantage of displacing the questions of construction and realization, so as to inscribe them within another dimension, one that is more strictly historical.

I will cite only one example: Rem Koolhaas's design for the Bibliothèque Nationale de France, the "Très Grande Bibliothèque." A title ("Très Grande Bibliothèque") that in itself posits an entire program, one that is almost Babelian. But a design (Koolhaas's) that seems illegible, at least when judged solely in terms of representation. Just as, at first encounter, the articulation between the model and the sectional views presented to us seems illegible. But that is because it was left to each individual to perform in turn, on their own initiative, work that the competition jurors did not realize they had to do, or that they were unable to do, caught, stuck as they were—the design they selected demonstrates this—in what Rem Koolhaas delights in calling the "semantic nightmare" of architecture. This design (Koolhaas's) will come to be seen, I dare say, as one of the great designs of the century's final years, one of those that most profoundly regenerates our idea of architecture. It merits this status not because of its proposed image of a library—Dominique Perrault shilled for his competition-winning design by describing it as "a library for France and a public square for Paris": as though a library should be a public square and a public square could function as a library—but because of the fiction it enforces of a *built* void, one inscribed within its very architectural volumes, the latter having been ripped or perforated by it through and through. As in another design, one that likewise now figures in the collection of Centre de Création Industrielle (CCI), the one by Norman Foster for the Hong Kong & Shanghai Bank in Hong Kong. And as in, already, a very beautiful design that one would also like to see enter this collection, the one by Jean Prouvé for the National Education Ministry, which was to have been built at La Défense but which miscarried—in one of those failures endemic in ill-comprehending democracies—thanks to the bureaucrats assigned to oversee its construction. These three designs—only one of which was built—constituting a series or group of transformations that has paradigmatic value.[25]

The CCI collection includes a few fragments by Jean Prouvé that are essentially structural in nature, like those deemed appropriate for nineteenth-century museums. We might regard as symbolic the absence, the lack, of this great design, itself built around a central void, the tower's central core having been subdivided and relegated to the building's four corners. Inside-out architecture, if you will, like a good deal of earlier modern architecture, and, like it, of interest to readers of Borges. An architecture such as we might have hoped for had things played out differently, if not in the National Education Ministry, then in the new Bibliothèque Nationale de France. Reduced as we are, momentarily, to Babel, we can only reread "Aleph" and dream, if not of the library then at least of the museum now being planned, hoping that, like a painting produced in accordance with Delacroix's views, it will retain something of the freedom of its preparatory sketch.

PART TWO

AMERICA
AS
SCENE

6

The Scene of Life of the Future

Upon returning to France from the United States at the end of the 1920s, Georges Duhamel published a book whose title— *Scenes from the Life of the Future*, which accurately reflects its tone —partly explains its success.[1] Had not America long been (isn't it still, but for how much longer?) the site of a fiction, even of the fiction par excellence, the one in which men turn away from that past that has shaped their identities to explore a future seemingly at odds with the very idea of permanence? I will appropriate this title here for my own purposes, excepting its plural form; for where Duhamel, in order to convey the horror and fear instilled in him by what he saw in the United States, chose to describe, as so many *scenes* (in the plural), a certain number of "things seen," from a visit to the slaughterhouses of Chicago to a movie screening in New York (both of which struck him as manifesting the same annihilative enterprise), what interests me here is how the United States—and, by metonymy, America itself—has come, during the last two centuries, to function as *one* scene. A scene, in the singular, onto which much of humanity, and not only that of Europe, has projected and continues to project its hopes, dreams, and desires, even its utopias, as well as the obsessions, nightmares, dreams, and fantasies of all kinds that have shaped, and continue to instigate, the enigma of its own destiny. To project these dreams and fantasies and stage them, incarnate them in multiple and contradictory figures. This entails the devising of sets, the casting of the roles, and above all the existence of a *scene* with a determinate structure, one whose operation is consistent with certain presuppositions and constraints: beginning with the fact that this scene can exist and function as such only if it presents itself as the scene of life of the future—of the same future that, by being thus staged, thus represented, constitutes itself.

To illustrate the kind of projective mechanism I have in mind, I turn to a document that, while neglected by historians, is nonetheless valuable as symptom: the message that Karl Marx sent to Abraham Lincoln on December 30, 1864, on behalf of the Workers' International, to congratulate him for having been reelected as president of the Union States. A war cry, and a cry of triumph: "Death to slavery!" According to the text of this letter, although the American War of Independence was the starting shot for the rise of the middle classes, the war against slavery opened the way for the revolt of the working classes. As Marx wrote in the letter's conclusion, the said working classes

consider it an earnest of the epoch to come that it fell to the lot of Abraham Lincoln, the single-minded son of the working class, to lead the country through the matchless struggle for the rescue of an enchained race and the reconstruction of a social world.[2]

The same text makes a point of celebrating the anticipatory example of "revolutionary defeatism" provided by the English working class, which, it is claimed, unstintingly supported the struggle of the States of the Union despite the many hardships resulting from the blockade, and especially from the cotton embargo.

At first glance, this letter appears to have no truck with either myth or dream: it contains not the slightest allusion to the notion of America as the Promised Land for all the disinherited of Europe, nor to democracy as described by Tocqueville. Even so, it is the earliest example of the investment of revolutionary ideology in a struggle, if not anti-imperialist, than at least anticolonialist, whose agents define their objectives in completely different terms. Throughout the twentieth century, Marxists of all kinds have deluded themselves about the "revolutionary" implications of national liberation movements, but Marx himself was not fooled by the language he had to use for propagandistic reasons; he was perfectly aware of what he called the "limited" character of the American Revolution. Something that, in his view, was demonstrated by the unequivocal, and apparently considered, response from Lincoln, conveyed by the American ambassador; specifically, by its assertion that the cause of the United States was not that of any single class but that of "human nature" itself.[3]

No allusions here, as I said, to the "Promised Land." Nonetheless, the letter from the Workers' International invokes a theme or feature decidedly calculated to appeal to the imagination: the vast unspoiled reaches of the territory of the United States, lands yet to be conquered, and that would be so not by troops of slaves but by free immigrants. The territorial dimension of what was then understood as the American scene had long since been grasped by Chateaubriand, who in his *Voyage en Amérique* writes of its "moral" import: "Finally, the United States has another safeguard: its population occupies less than an eighteenth of its territory. America still dwells in solitude; for some time yet her wilderness will be her manners, and her enlightenment her liberty."[4] This formulation would find its political translation, if we credit the analysis proposed by Marx and Engels in their articles for the *New York Daily Tribune*, in the Republicans' declared intention, which was at the root of the Civil War, to confine slavery to the territories in which it was legal, whereas the slave system could be maintained only on the condition—according to Marx, an "economic law"—that it expand indefinitely.[5]

The question was especially critical insofar as it pertained to the ideology of the "frontier," in its specifically American sense. For Europeans, frontiers are what separate two states, corresponding to boundaries between two entities of like logical status. As defined by the American historian Frederick Jackson Turner,[6] however, the word designates a limit that, by its very nature, must continuously be advanced, between an area in which savagery has been conquered and one in which it prevails, even as it (the edge of the frontier) corresponds to a constantly shifting border between the full and the empty, the cultivated and the uncultivated, light and darkness. All of which corresponds rather well to the definition of a *scene* in the theatrical sense: such a playing area is not separated from its context by a border, but by a line that delimits it and constitutes it as such, in the same way that a figure stands out against a background that it can, *at the limit*, come to occupy fully.

In the matter of figures, Marx's letter to Lincoln evokes not only the theater of history but also the actors that perform in it: players of a new kind who cannot be described as "heroes," unless we understand the word in an explicitly "modern" sense. According to Marx, "Never yet has the New World scored a greater victory than in this instance, through its demonstration that, thanks to its political and social organization, ordinary people of good will can carry out tasks which the Old World would have to have a hero to accomplish!" To play the role assigned him by history, Lincoln, like Washington, had no need to wear an antique mask and drape himself in a toga, like the actors in the French Revolution. If, as Hegel maintained, comedy is superior to tragedy, just as humor and reasoned irony are superior to pathos, then Lincoln is the right hero for America. For "if Lincoln does not possess the gift of the pathos of historic action, he does as an ordinary man, coming from the people, possess the gift of the humor of that action."[7]

According to Marx (still), the roles assigned by the classical tradition to those it designates "great men" will shrink as economic conditions mature: Chateaubriand, again, understood clearly the differing stature of the two figures that Providence had placed at the head of the destiny of their respective centuries, Napoleon and Washington. Marx would claim that the conditions of bourgeois revolution in the United States did not cry out for a Napoleon, that it had no need for a strong state capable of destroying a precapitalist structure, since none such existed there. In his own distinctive language, Chateaubriand had previously noted the different kinds of ambition characteristic of those he presented as the *actors* of contemporary history. Washington did not move on "a vast stage," however extensive his field of operations, at least virtually; he was not "confronted" by great captains and powerful monarchs; he did not dream of "upsetting thrones." His ambition, unlike that of the man Chateaubriand insisted on calling Bonaparte, was *modern* in every sense of the word, and with all that this implied in the way of historical amnesia: he defended himself, with a handful of citizens, in a land without fame and without memories. But both figures were to be rewarded according to their deserts: Bonaparte's empire was destroyed, but Washington's Republic still exists, and his name is associated with the beginning of a new era for mankind.[8]

Thus did Chateaubriand, and Marx after him, set the scene and summon forth the actors. But it is Tocqueville who must be credited with having acknowledged the value of America (or the USA, as Le Corbusier would call it in the next century) as "model." Paradoxically, this country without a past, this country without memory, this "new" country, presented itself, in the political order, as a prefiguration of the future—at least of a possible future—of European societies, the "American project" per se revealing itself only within the context of the projections to which it lent itself, and of which it was perhaps a product. The progressive development of equality and democracy seemed an irreversible given, an ineluctable fact, "providential," as Tocqueville put it. America being the country in which this great revolution—for such it appeared to Europeans who had pondered the end of the old regime—had reached its natural limit (here again we encounter the idea of *limit*, associated this time, characteristically, with nature), as well as a nation that saw the results of this revolution without having experienced revolution itself, insofar as the new order was not obliged to rise from the ruins of a preexisting order. Sooner or later—such was Tocqueville's view—Europe would achieve, like America, conditions of almost complete social equality:

I have acknowledged this revolution as a fact already accomplished, or on the eve of its accomplishment; and I have selected the nation, from among those which have undergone it, in which its development has been the most peaceful and the most complete, in order to discern its natural consequences and to find out, if possible, the means of rendering it profitable to mankind. I confess that in America I saw more than America; I sought there the image of democracy itself, with its inclinations, its character, its prejudices, and its passions, in order to learn what we have to fear or to hope from its progress.[9]

The great question, for Tocqueville, was whether liberty could be reconciled with equality, and whether we should aim for a liberal republic or an aggressive one, for freedom or democratic tyranny. In his view, America had solved this problem by accepting the principle of the sovereignty of the people and by applying it in the most direct, unlimited, and absolute way; which sufficed to make its people the most prosperous and most stable on earth, thereby proving that the republic could and should be the guardian of all rights, beginning with that of property, which Tocqueville regarded as a key foundation of liberty, and even of equality.

Where else could we find greater causes of hope, or more instructive lessons? Let us look to America, not in order to make a servile copy of the institutions that she has established, but to gain a clearer view of the polity that will be the best for us; let us look there less to find examples than instruction; let us borrow from her the principles, rather than the details, of her laws. The laws of the French republic may be, and ought to be in many cases, different from those which govern the United States; but the principles on which the American constitutions rest, those principles of order, of the balance of powers, of true liberty, of deep and sincere respect for right, are indispensable to all republics; they ought to be common to all; and it may be said beforehand that wherever they are not found, the republic will soon have ceased to exist.[10]

There is, however, another side to the medal. As evidenced—to cite but one example—by the attitude of Americans toward the arts: "Democratic nations . . . will cultivate the arts that serve to render life easy in preference to those whose object is to adorn it."

In a society which holds that the practice of the arts is a privilege, and that the arts themselves are a matter of concern only for the privileged few, craftsmen will no longer worry about quality, preferring instead to turn out as quickly as possible things that can be sold at the lowest possible price. In addition to directing the human spirit toward the useful arts, Democracy encourages craftsmen to make flawed products quickly and consumers to make do with them. Grandeur being out of the question, they aim for elegance and prettiness. Appearance takes precedence over reality. Raising the stakes in advance over Marx's statement that the bourgeoisie prefers luxury to beauty, Tocqueville proposed a formulation that is even more striking: "The hypocrisy of virtue is of every age; but the hypocrisy of luxury belongs more particularly to the ages of democracy."[11] And, in addition, what boredom, as Stendhal would say (although he never went to America, he must have read Tocqueville): in aristocratic societies,

the man who approaches a Court compromises his happiness, if he is happy, and in any case risks making his future depend on the intrigues of some chambermaid. On the other hand, in America, in the Republic, one must waste a whole day in paying serious court to the shopkeepers in the streets, and must become as stupid as they are; and over there, no opera.[12]

Regarding this last point, at least, history has proven Stendhal wrong. But his error offers me an occasion to evoke, in passing, a matter that has some bearing on my argument. Of the architects made famous by the rebuilding of Chicago after the great fire of 1871, and who are often presented as the creators—unknown to themselves—of a new "structural" architecture,[13] as the first champions of a "functionalist" aesthetic, at least two were great opera lovers. John Welborn Root, regarded by William Condit as one of the four principal American architects, along with H. H. Richardson, Louis H. Sullivan, and Frank Lloyd Wright, divided his time, at the beginning of his Chicago career, between architecture and music criticism. And Sullivan himself, who was to build the famous auditorium destined to house the Lyric Opera of Chicago (obliged in the meantime, for a period of several years, to perform in the open air), was a committed Wagnerite. Which might seem surprising on the part of the author of the celebrated observation that "form follows function," if we consider the nature of the Wagnerian theater or *scene*, and the divorce it implies between the real and the ideal, between technical function and scenic effect.[14]

To return to Tocqueville, I want to stress two points. On the one hand, the value he attributes to America as example or model, at least theoretically, and his belief that it offers European societies an image of their own future. On the other hand, his position that, while laws can vary from one country to another, their principles, by contrast, are universal, legal universalism being reconcilable with actual particularism or regionalism. Which brings us to Tocqueville's notion that the gradual development of equality has every appearance of being "divinely ordained": it is universal, it is lasting, it eludes human control; all the elements, and all men, concur in it and serve it. A sign that, if America presents itself as the very image of the future, that is because it is a point of culmination, a mature form achieved at the end of a seemingly natural process.

One hundred years after Tocqueville, Georges Duhamel still saw America as a prefiguration of the world's future. But his reaction to this was one of horror. Liberty versus democratic tyranny: this debate became moot as soon as America became smitten with preceding the rest of humanity down the route of dreadful experiments, and with the subjection imposed by a social apparatus without parallel elsewhere: a monstrous phantom, a constraining aggregate of laws, institutions, myths, and prejudices; a system in which individuals were enslaved not so much by a political and social regimen as by moralists (prohibition was then at its height), lawmakers, hygienists, doctors (it was as a doctor that Duhamel had been invited there), urbanists, and even aestheticians, policemen, publicists, jazz, money, the movies. To be sure, Duhamel's tone is very different from that of Tocqueville. But America functions in much the same way in both of their texts. In fact, what might be called

the voyage-to-America literary genre would not have enjoyed even
the equivocal success with which we are familiar if its basic thrust
had not been projective, and if the country's character as "model"
had not acquired a mythic dimension, one that is even dreamlike,
fantasmatic. Something that characterized it from the start, and
which becomes confounded with the birth of French literature, when
Montaigne—in the middle of Book I of the *Essays*—ponders the
implications of the recent discovery of a new world, supposedly "infinite," comparing the mores of its inhabitants to our own.[15] Stendhal did likewise, and at the very moment Tocqueville invited his
readers to rediscover America. The invention of modern literature
likewise proceeded by way—a way ever open—of the new continent. Consider Kafka, who traveled there only in imagination but
whose novel *Amerika* has lost none of its pertinence, precisely because of its fantastic character.

America is not merely a dream, good or bad; it functions as a
projection of the unconscious: better still, as the incarnate, realized
unconscious of a Europe troubled by its antiquity, real and imagined, with all that this implies on its side in the way of resistance
and repression. It presents at least one constitutive trait of the unconscious, if we hold, with Freud, that the unconscious has no history. The notion that America—"juvenile" America, as Le Corbusier called it—has no history, nor even a past, is in effect another
fantasy of "old" Europe, one that becomes confused with the fantasy of modernity in its European version. No history, and—so it is
claimed; but the two go together—no art, no monuments.

It was long taken for granted that America had no art. Tocqueville thought this was self-evident, but his view was a function
of his knowing, or believing that he knew, in 1828, what "art" was,
like those who repeated this commonplace in the 1920s and 1930s.
Today the question takes on another cast, with rising prices in the
art market having put things right. But how could the questions
that now preoccupy us have mattered to Tocqueville? His concern
was to discover *why some of the monuments erected by Americans are
so mean whereas others are so grand.*

In a democratic community individuals are very powerless; but the State which represents them all and contains them all within its grasp, is very powerful. . . . [In democratic states] the imagination of men is compressed when men consider themselves; it expands indefinitely when they think of the State. Hence it is that the same men who live on a small scale in narrow dwellings frequently aspire to gigantic splendor in the erection of their public monuments.[16]

And Tocqueville evokes the way that Americans had traced on the site of their capital city the *walls* [*l'enceinte*] of an immense city, one that, when he was writing, boasted a population scarcely larger than that of Pontoise. In other words, an imaginary metropolis. As though, once again, the scene had been set, or rather sketched in advance, but in a way distinctly at odds with the language used by Tocqueville, who here employed a very European term. American cities, of course, have no walls that must be negotiated in the process of expansion. Like the American scene generally, they exemplify another mode of implantation, one whose regulatory template is the infinitely expandable grid.

But what could be the meaning of "monument" in a country declared by Chateaubriand to be without a past, without memory, unless the notion be separated from that of memory? As we read in *The Natchez*: "The Europeans had as yet no tombs in America when they already had dungeons. These were the only monuments of the past for this society without ancestors and without memories." The prison as monument to the past—the only past that such a society could acknowledge, one linked to error and crime? The notion of an American scene here approaches paradox and contradiction; for while American cities lacked "monuments . . . churches and houses embellished with the columns of Greek architecture" these could be found, by contrast, in the middle of the woods and along riverbanks, "antique ornaments in the desert." But let us read more carefully, or a bit farther along:

Protestantism, which makes no offerings to imagination and is itself new, has not raised those towers and domes with which the old Catholic religion has crowned Europe. Almost nothing in Philadelphia, New York, and Boston rises above the mass of walls and roofs. This flatness saddens the eye.[17]

Here again, of course, things have changed considerably. At present, it is old Europe and China, older still, that worry about the proliferation of skyscrapers on their soil, much as Montaigne's contemporaries pondered the arrival of "cannibals" in Paris. Could they survive there? If they reproduced, how quickly would their number grow? It is nonetheless symptomatic that Chateaubriand was able to adduce, in 1828, the traversal of, or rather the retreat from, another frontier, another limit: one not horizontal but regarding height. This limit would soon be exceeded, or rather extended, by monuments of a new kind, a new type. Monuments not to the past but to the future, monuments of modernity, and of a modernity little indebted to the past, despite its dressing itself up in columns, pinnacles, and pediments. Everything in this scene, on this stage, was to speak of the future, including its very structure: there were not, there could no longer be any monuments save those to the future, just as there was not, nor could be, any tradition other than—to quote Harold Rosenberg—that of *the new*.[18] And the skyscraper bears the imprint of this, tending ineluctably, naturally, as if with divine sanction, to surpass itself: a self-surpassing that must be described as structural, in the sense that, if any structural system can be assigned a limit height, a point of catastrophe (René Thom's phrase: twenty-five floors for a conventional concrete structure) beyond which everything will collapse, one need only change this structural system to proceed further, to build higher.

Immediately after disembarking from the Normandy in 1935, Le Corbusier announced to stunned journalists that the skyscrapers of New York were too small. As for Frank Lloyd Wright (who a year later, at the first Congress of Soviet Architects, held in Moscow at the height of the Stalinist purge, urged his listeners not to imitate what he called "official" American architecture, especially the skyscraper, "the tomb of architecture"),[19] he eventually envisioned a tower of two thousand floors, a design for which engineers in Chicago are currently trying to devise a viable structural system. The

American scene, America as scene, is this, too: a scene, a stage, whose scale is dreamlike, utopian; one whose structures are infinite in number, and that seem always to hold something in reserve, to the point that it appears conceivable, at least in theory, *to make history with structure.*

I have used the term "utopia"; and America, of course, is a utopia that has been *realized,* if only in part, or not entirely as originally envisioned. What did Le Corbusier hope to find there? Proofs, and an example: "I am going to show through the USA, taken as an example, that the times are new but that its living quarters are uninhabitable."[20] America, the USA, as "proof." And first of all as technical proof, proof that utopia is effectively realizable: one can build to great heights because of the working elevators there (the same elevators that Duhamel detested), and because skyscrapers hold their own against the wind. But also as ideological proof, proof that a utopian scale has its pertinence: skyscrapers set the scale for a new era. Now this change of scale presented itself as a specifically "American" trait, one that did not fail to impress early travelers (one need only remember Chateaubriand's description of the confluence of the Mississippi and Missouri rivers) long before the appearance of the first skyscrapers.

We will dwell here on only one of aspect among many. Le Corbusier considered New York to be an urban catastrophe, but a "fairy catastrophe." Likewise, the skyscraper was an architectural catastrophe, but one that he nonetheless regarded as architecture, and even beautiful architecture, going so far as to call them "levers of hope." This dimension, this scale, which I, too, will call "catastrophic," is specific to the American scene, just as it is specific to a certain modernity, haunted as the latter has always been—even before the appearance of the atom bomb on the stage of history—by the threat of an always possible apocalypse. Long before films like *Towering Inferno* and the many articles regularly published in the American press on the impending threat of powerful hurricanes and the questionable stability of tall buildings, Jules Verne managed to assemble and stage the various elements of the myth in a novel that was like-

wise anticipatory, *A Floating City*. The crossings of the Great Eastern, an immense passenger liner built in the United States for transatlantic voyages, had been marred by a series of serious accidents,
and many travelers preferred to take European "clippers," which
were smaller but also faster: an early case of the Concorde versus the
747. But the terms were set, and from the start: a change of scale was
established even before travelers had set foot on America soil. And
along with this change of scale, an inherent dimension of catastrophe, accompanied by a constant anticipation rife with narrative pos-
sibilities. In fact, the catastrophe never arrives (this isn't the movies),
and the protagonists, after disembarking, are obliged to visit Niagara
Falls to find themselves confronted by a catastrophe of another kind,
a natural one that strikes them as sublime: thanks to which the beautiful Ellen, who had been suffering from amnesia, recovers her memory, which in this context amounts in itself to an entire program. For
the young woman certainly could not have recovered her memory in
New York. A city that, in its form, its physical appearance (according to Jules Verne) was quickly seen: "It is hardly more varied than a
checkerboard," the author declares straight-out—despite never having seen it. (In *The Begum's Fortune*, Verne comes closer to acknowl-
edging the specifically scenic functions of the grid, the story being
premised on an opposition between two models or types of regular
plan: a circular and concentric one, declared Germanic and oppressive, much like Bentham's panoptikon; and a regular orthogonal
grid, pronounced French and democratic).

Thus the American myth or "dream," if not the American
"nightmare," presents itself in multiple, often contradictory guises
in which archaism contends—the paradox is now more apparent
than ever, to the point of occasionally tragic caricature—with modernism.[21] To say nothing of its more or less pronounced individual
connotations. To be sure, the image of America cannot be reduced
to the skyscraper, and everyone can conjure in his or her mind photographs by Stieglitz and Lewis Hine showing immigrants crammed
together on the deck of a ship or waiting their turn at Ellis Island,
and Farm Security Administration photographs showing an Amer-

ica in crisis (and decidedly on the margins of modernity, however the term is understood), views that are now part of universal iconography: everyone encounters them at one time or another, whether or not they have occasion to cross the Atlantic. And that is exactly what most troubled Duhamel: the grip that America already had on the imaginary—and this at a time when the Hollywood machine was just gearing up—and against which do-gooders periodically feigned, as they still do today, to protest. A little anti-Americanism always comes in handy for those out to assert, at little cost, their independence and authority, whether political or institutional.

If architecture, as opposed to the "American way of life," as opposed to movies or television, assumes particular importance in this context, that is because it is a reliable indicator of the problems associated with modernity. A unique indicator: although we certainly didn't need the Americans to explain to us that architecture is a matter of *construction*, "American" scale has a preeminently technological dimension (Le Corbusier: "Listen to American engineers, not the architects!"). But also a political or social indicator: in today's China, architecture functions as one of the most visible instruments —if not the most visible—of "modernization," ostensibly proving to the world and the Chinese masses that the Chinese can be "modern," that they know how to build and maintain very tall buildings. And this on one of the premier stages of international capitalism, in the very heart of Hong Kong. Whereas in Nankin (the capital of China under Japanese occupation) peasants from the surrounding area come to see the Jingling Hotel, a monument to modernity—or should we say modernization?—set aside for foreigners and situated smack in the center of the old city, its forty stories towering above the surrounding low houses.

Not only skyscrapers, of course, are in question: American architecture compels our attention for other reasons as well. It is not a matter of chance that the premier president of the United States was an architect, and that he explicitly exhorted his compatriots to *build democracy*: Jefferson, widely regarded as the representative par excellence of agrarian ideology, and who saw farmers as the surest bulwark of democracy, this man of the Enlightenment also delighted in city lights: quite literally, if it is true that Philadelphia, which boasted 70,000 inhabitants in 1800, was then better paved and illuminated than London. In truth, Jefferson never focused on American cities, concentrating his attacks instead on European ones, which he saw as cesspools of vice, whereas crime, according to him, was unknown in the country. Although he never explicitly discussed in his writings the relation between industrial development and the character of European cities as reservoirs of manpower and concentrations of the poor, awareness of such a relation is implicit in the horror with which he regarded the Industrial Revolution and even manufacturing, which he could accept only half-heartedly, and then only to prevent a weakening of the power of the United States.

In fact, throughout the nineteenth century it was America that never ceased looking toward Europe, and first of all toward urban Europe, that of the industrial cities described by Engels in *The Condition of the Working Classes in England*, and soon toward the metropolises that were the preferred objects of study of German sociology at the end of the century: beginning with Georg Simmel, whose work was quite influential in the United States, whereas only now are we beginning to discover him in France. In an important book, Morton and Lucia White have studied the emergence of what they call an antiurban ideology in the Unites States contemporary with the transformation of America's colonial into large metropolises, which began to flourish only after the Civil War.[22] It seems clear that American intellectuals did not view cities as we do, as places where a culture is born and nurtured. Instead, they saw them as evidence of a break with a specifically American "past," as images of a savagery quite different from that of the wilderness in which American man had first learned to survive, and which indeed had appeared to him as a refuge. Thoreau's Walden was now countered by Poe's man of the crowd, an individual who cannot bear solitude and is most at home in the midst of multitudes. As for the protagonist of Melville's *Pierre, or the Ambiguities*, before he can face the city (and literature), he must spend the night under the enormous rock he associates with his childhood, much as, for many years, the Kaufmanns left their offices in Pittsburgh every week and headed for the house nestling in the little vale of Bear Run, in the Pennsylvania forest, that Frank Lloyd Wright had built for them. The roots of this antiurban ideology, which indeed left its mark on American culture, were not exclusively agrarian and anarchist: it sprung to an equal extent from the horror inspired by the example of the European city, which then seemed to prefigure a dreaded future. For Melville, Hawthorne, and Henry Adams, the scenes of the life of the future were to be found in Europe: in London, Liverpool, and even Rome.

The face of the American city was soon to change. In 1830, Chicago had a mere 4,000 inhabitants, but by 1850 its population had grown to 30,000, reaching 300,000 by 1870, 500,000 by 1880, 1,100,000 by 1890, and two million by 1900, attaining seven million by 1960.[23] Making this a city that, within the span of a single lifetime, grew from a settlement of a few buildings to one of the world's great urban centers, and one whose identity as such would be strengthened by a new architecture (one whose novelty derived not only from the skyscraper but also from grain silos, which greatly impressed Gropius and Le Corbusier). A city whose development was perceived, by those who simultaneously effected and witnessed it, as "divinely ordained," in Tocqueville's sense, and as a natural, even catastrophic, process. One is reminded here of the character in Pasternak's *Doctor Zhivago* who lies down in the grass to watch it grow, for Alexander Hesler, who arrived in Chicago in 1853, did much the same thing. His panoramic daguerreotypes, taken year after year from the top of the courthouse, constitute a visible record of the irresistible growth of the new metropolis, even before the fire of 1871.[24] Theodore Dreiser, who also got his start in Chicago, was among the first to describe the city as spectacle, as scene. As for Knut Hamsun, whose visit to the United States in the 1880s resulted in a ferocious book on the nation's cultural life, he denounced the reduction of literature there to a form of "journalism": he had to acknowledge that, despite its faults, the press was the most authentic and most serious cultural manifestation of the American people—and, in literary terms, thanks to its audacity and its violent realism, the most modern one.[25] In the same sense, Dreiser liked to say that neither sociology nor scientific analysis interested him. He wanted to be not a sociologist but a writer, or at the very least a journalist; what mattered to him, he repeated, was describing, *seeing*.[26]

Now it was precisely by taking journalistic practice as a model that the first school of urban sociology constituted itself in Chicago.[27] Its founder, Robert Ezra Park, conceived of the sociologist as a kind of super-reporter whose job it was to reconstitute, using what he called "life stories," the variety of social types brought together in the great "social laboratory" of the city—an "existential" approach to urban reality being at one here with a quasi-naturalist vision of the urban milieu, of its mobility and transmutability, always considered in relation to specific spatial context. The resulting studies—for example, Louis Wirth's famous book on the ghetto, or the concentric developmental model of Chicago elaborated by Park and Burgess, who revealed how new immigrants arriving in the city center repeatedly pushed those who had preceded them toward the periphery, while its monied classes had chosen from the beginning to reside in what, from the 1850s, were known as *suburbs*—these studies of social chemistry and topography could not fail to attract the attention of the French master of social morphology, Maurice Halbwachs. If I dwell on them here, it is because they bear directly, through the example of Chicago, on the "scene" under discussion: a scene of human life that encompasses its *future* development.

To travel, to visit foreign lands, is to give oneself the world as representation, to see others as actors. Frenchmen arriving today in Beijing or Shanghai effectively claim for themselves the right to "stage," for strictly personal ends, hundreds, even thousands of Chinese; who of course couldn't care less. Until the moment when the spectator, the person experiencing the spectacle, senses that he is himself being observed, shoved onto a stage about which he knows virtually nothing. But how would this have played out in a city like Chicago, beginning in 1850, populated as it was, to a great extent,

by more or less newly arrived immigrants: in a word by *foreigners*?
The foreigner whom Georg Simmel, in a now classic study, posited
as the paradigmatic example of the "objective man," the distance he
keeps from the group in which he finds himself making of him the
indicator—and, simultaneously, the *analyzer*—par excellence of social mobility within the morphological boundaries of an urban milieu that his multiplied presence suffices to constitute as a scene,
without there being any need for an exterior gaze.[28] On the scene of
future life, every individual is simultaneously actor and spectator,
spectator and actor, while awaiting his or her *naturalization*, less in
an institutional than an evolutionary or even taxidermic sense of the
word. But this wait is itself implicated in the scene, which conditions it through and through.

What I am trying to pin down here, tentatively, is the moment America constituted itself, in its own eyes, as a scene on which
it dreaded having to recognize itself for what it was. A moment of
fascination mixed with repulsion, and one that led to a deepening of
the work of the Chicago school of urban ecology. But a moment as
well, correlatively, of disenchantment in the face of an evolution
that seemed to escape all control, despite being as strictly programmed as any natural process could be. A disenchantment that,
in combination with a realization that European cities had themselves been changed by state intervention, led to the establishment
of the City Beautiful movement, whose goal was the a posteriori
beautification of the metropolis. The members of a commission established in 1900—the year of the International Exposition in Paris
—at the initiative of Senator James McMillan (Daniel Burnham,
the Chicago architect; Charles McKim, another architect based on
the East Coast; Frederick Law Olmsted Jr., the man of national and
urban parks, beginning with Central Park in New York; and the
sculptor Augustus Saint Gaudens) embarked on a study trip that
took them to Vienna, Budapest, Paris, Rome, Frankfurt, and London, after which they submitted a proposal for the "beautification"
of Washington, D.C., about which one can only say that there was
nothing new, much less "modern," about it.

The image and myth of America played such a decisive role in the crystallization of modernist ideology in Europe that it is a matter of some importance to understand clearly the equivocal nature of the relation, in the early twentieth century, between America as the scene of life of the future and America as the scene of modernity. A strictly ideological conjuncture, and one in many respects illusory, like the no less equivocal disjunction today between the dimension of the future and that of modernity, as signaled by the new metonymic displacement, from whole to part, whereby, within the American scene, California is now the *scene of life of the future*, but of a future life no longer consistent with accepted definitions of modernity, corresponding instead to a way of life dubbed "postmodern." Which definition—another paradox—imposed itself in the United States only because an unforeseeable graft permitted a few European masters of the modern movement to play a role on the American stage. After a twenty- or thirty-year game of hide-and-seek whose complexity is only now becoming clear, aptly summed up by Le Corbusier's remark that the Americans had managed to achieve what "we" wanted to, but improperly, catastrophically (although he deemed the phenomenon a "fairy catastrophe"), the arrival in the United States, on the eve of World War II, of the masters of the Bauhaus, from Gropius to Mies Van der Rohe, ultimately had the effect, in the American context, of imposing a singularly restrictive notion of modernity, one unwilling and unable to profit from the achievements of a specifically American modernity whose secret agenda is only now being revealed after having long been obscured by misleading public-relations pronouncements, as we shall see later through the example of what Rem Koolhaas has called "Manhattanism."

The Europeans have been paid back, for the debate about modernity that now occupies center stage was programmed in its entirety, again, by the American example or "model." But an example or model, this time, pertinent only to the American scene. After functioning for more than two centuries as the scene of the life of the future, America effectively acquired a past: a past borrowed in part, and linked to the above-mentioned modernist graft, which took with wondrous effectiveness. Today America affects to reject this graft, imitated in this by old Europe. The problem is that the tree from which the branch was taken has not borne quite the same fruit in Europe, and that detaching it in hopes of becoming up-to-date and perhaps moving onto the scene of the future entails some risk of becoming still more outmoded, and a bit more nostalgic. Just as today in New York—a "vertical" city, as Le Corbusier said, but one that nonetheless remains, in many respects, the "horizontal" city described by Paul Morand[29]—one finds oneself on the scene of a "future" so rife with memories that no one seems much inclined to do without them. A completely "modern" future, despite its already belonging to the past, whereas the modernity that it proclaims, marked as it is—and always has been—by multiple archaic traits, has little to do with the one about which the European imagination continues to fantasize.

Which raises a question: What if America is not merely the formidable reservoir of myths, forms, and images, also of fetishized fashions, objects, and products that we are pleased to take it for? What if these myths, these forms, these images owe something of their power, their empire, to their character as exports, to the way they let us glimpse the plays of opposition that have shaped them without ever completely reconciling or surmounting them, retaining them, rather, in all their virulence? Something they manage to do (such is my hypothesis) solely because of their constitutive relation with the American scene: either because these myths, objects, and images remain forever associated with the American landscape, as this term is generally understood (something that could also be said of the skyscraper); or because they are among its determinant elements (likewise true of the skyscraper).

Passing as it often does, in the most abrupt way, from horizontal to vertical, from dilution to concentration, from dissemination to congestion, the process of urbanization characteristic of America is worth examining. For while the word can be used, yet again, without necessarily giving it the dramatic connotations it often has in the writings of Le Corbusier, America, from the moment it operates constantly, and in the most spectacular way, as a pivot between two opposing and even contradictory regimens, presents itself as a site of *catastrophe* (according to René Thom, there is "catastrophe" wherever there is phenomenological discontinuity—for example, a passage without transition, in the form of a right angle, from horizontal to vertical[30]). The American example or model, not to say "Americanism" in all its many forms and guises, being most virulent when it imposes on "European consciousness," more or less surreptitiously, a change of regimen that unsettles it, that puts it in motion, that *moves* it in its solidmost phenomenal foundations: here again, America functions as the unconscious of Europe.

I illustrate this assertion with the following three experiences.

1. *Aerial perspective.* Arrival in Chicago, via Montreal, late on a winter afternoon: as the plane descends, the moment, in the dazzle of the setting sun, where the grand lines of the urban fabric seem to melt into the Jeffersonian grid of the broad western plains stretching to the horizon, a pattern even imprinted on the snow. The aerial perspective of the plan by Daniel Burnham and Edward Bennet for greater Chicago (1909), represented in watercolor drawings by Jules Guérin, is rather consistent with this inscription of the city on the land. Except that the grid of the city center accommodates a starburst of radiating thoroughfares, while the Loop, which even today circles the first cast-iron-and-steel vertical city like a lasso, is here effectively "untied" and made to resemble a winding riverbed, becoming an integral part of the monumental and geographic configuration of the "Paris of the Great Plains" conceived by these good students of the École des Beaux-Arts. And as for the yellow band stretching from one end to the other of the horizon, if it evokes, paradoxically, sunrise as much as sunset, this reversal of orientation is consistent with the idea of the "frontier," continually pushed back in the course of the march westward. *In America, the Orient*—in all senses of the word, including the Far East, China and Japan—*is in the west.*

2. *Skyline.* Leaving, this time, the Dallas-Fort Worth airport,

International Parkway heads into a vast deserted plain exactly half-way between the two cities, as indicated by two signs flanking the crossroads: at right, "Dallas, 20 miles"; at left, "Fort Worth, 20 miles." Of my arrival in Dallas, I remember only a morass of hang-ars and huge shopping centers with restaurants and movie theaters. At the time (1986), the Hyatt Hotel rose in isolation somewhere be-tween the desert and the urban agglomeration, as though keeping its distance from that latter so as not to compromise itself; but then its assertively modern, "high tech" architecture made a much greater effect in this no-man's-land than it would have in Dallas itself, an oddly discrete and elusive city whose points of architectural inter-est (for one thing, a small theater by Frank Lloyd Wright) are not immediately apparent. Things are very different in Fort Worth: ar-riving from Dallas on the arrow-straight turnpike, one is surprised to see the glittering skyline suddenly appear against the darkest night, the city merging into its own luminous sign thanks to mil-lions of electric light bulbs spaced regularly over the profiles of its skyscrapers. An effect reminiscent of Saul Steinberg (*The Discovery of America*), for the city seems to produce a two-dimensional draw-ing of itself.

3. *Manhattan.* Finally this, so banal that one would hesitate to describe it, if it weren't for the fact that the experience can no longer be taken for granted, that only through tourist networks (the Circle Line, a trip to Brooklyn Heights, the Staten Island Ferry, even a helicopter tour) can we now recover something of the emotional impact experienced by those who first saw Manhattan from steamer decks and airplane windows, in the years when ocean liners still got close to it. Today we have postcards, which record frontal and aerial views of Manhattan such as few tourists see, given that most must make do with the panoramas and more or less vertiginous views from the observation decks of the Empire State Building, Rocke-feller Center, and the World Trade Center. Such imagery compet-ing, in the confusion of the "real" and the "virtual" (think of the various uses to which the image of Manhattan is put in the movies), with the multiple views offered by the city itself.

Virtual: the image of the city has been this for some time, and not only in America. It's been quite a while since *vedute*, or silhouetted views of cities along rivers and enclosed by walls, were replaced by aerial views. As noted above, long before the invention of the hot-air balloon, men of art could, using graphic and projective means, fashion "bird's-eye" views in which the point of view, constantly shifting, seems to stretch toward infinity. When New York was still known as New Amsterdam, the Dutch painter Jan Micker painted a *View of Amsterdam* in which the network of canals is rendered less in the conventional planimetric way than as kind of axonometric plan *avant la lettre*, oriented with regard to a point situated somewhere below a screen of clouds casting shadows on the city.[31] Things were rather different on the island of Manhattan, despite a line of fortifications marking the settlement's northern limit, and despite the fact that Canal Street, now one of the city's most animated thoroughfares, often choked with traffic emerging from the Holland Tunnel, reminds us, through its name, that a few canals cut into the rock once serviced a number of boat slips at high tide: views of the first establishment of the East India Company on American soil are largely fantastic, the better to make them consistent, in plan as well as facade, with traditional images of cities on riverbanks and enclosed by walls, windmills occasionally having been added to complete the effect.[32]

It is true that much of the impact of modern Manhattan, much of its "aura," in Benjamin's sense, whether viewed frontally or from the air, derives from its monumental geometric outline, the invention of its skyline paralleling that of its site. The city's contours are as distinct in plan (the clear boundary between the island and the surrounding waters being tailor-made to seduce the Dutch) as they are in elevation: save that, far from being reducible to a silhouette, to a simple facade-effect, Manhattan stands out against the sky like a series of *profiles*, creating what Le Corbusier called a *"spectacle plastique."* Manhattan doesn't stare admiringly at itself in the water any more than Chicago does. But while the Chicago of Burnham and Bennet as pictured by Jules Guérin finds its reflection less

in Lake Michigan, which it fronts across a broad stretch in the fore-
ground, than in the grid of the plain to its west, the Narcissus
known as Manhattan, after having long multiplied openings onto
itself, gave itself the only mirror appropriate to it: the one offered by
its own architecture when it set out to compete with photomontages, in hopes of restoring the dynamic and contrasted image of
the metropolis of the future. Glass curtain-walls, used to such exemplary effect by Gordon Bunshaft in Lever House (by contrast
with other buildings, for example, Eero Saarinen's CBS tower, with
its rhythmic projecting elements faced in dark stone), reflect not
only the facades of neighboring buildings but the sky itself, as well
as passing clouds "pushed by the wind," to quote Antonio di Tucci
Manetti on the first perspective demonstration associated with the
name of Brunelleschi: a demonstration that itself responded to a
preeminently narcissistic drive insofar as it sought to replace the
gaze directed at the city with its mirror image. Which, here as there,
in Bunshaft's Manhattan as in Brunelleschi's Florence, entailed the
risk of Narcissus's dying a "symbolic" death, of his—to cite Ovid's
Metamorphoses—"perish[ing] through his own eyes."[33]

If I evoke here, yet again, Brunelleschi's experiments in the
form of demonstrations, it is because they relate to the question of
the subject, in the modern if not the Western sense of the word. The
subject, insofar as it is implicated, as the point of "origin," in the
perspective configuration, in the *punto dell'occhio* that corresponds
to the image of the point of view inscribed on the plane of projection, becoming indistinguishable from the so-called vanishing point.
But, likewise, the subject—they are one and the same, perspective
being directly related to architecture, and especially to that of the
city—implicated in the urban configuration as the preeminent site
within which it (the subject) exercises the functions proper to it, perhaps even as the site of its emergence.[34] The subject that was to be
so radically affected by the discovery of America, in the very year
(1492) that saw the death of that other great theorist of perspective,
Piero della Francesca. It is not only that Christopher Columbus,
motivated from the start by a trope characteristic of what would be-

come American culture, himself chose to take a westward route to reach the East. The discovery, along the way, of America's "savages" was to lead the Western subject, at precisely the moment it was endeavoring to constitute itself as such, to operate a first return onto itself, although one that was in no respect narcissistic: so true is it, as Rousseau would write (Montaigne said the same the thing), that "to study man one must look far and wide," and, "first, observe differences so as to discover particular qualities"—a formulation that, as is well known, Lévi-Strauss pronounced the founding act of anthropology; and one that the architect Adolf Loos made his own when he undertook, the first of his kind to do so, an American Grand Tour, creating, after returning to Vienna, a periodical of which only two issues appeared but whose title—*Das Andere*—implied a program.[35] Classical antiquity had its barbarians, which it did not acknowledge to be "men." Modern Europe was to have its "savages," a circumstance that led it to reconsider, under the sign of the Other, the notion of "humanity."

To varying degrees and in various guises, America has never ceased playing in the European imaginary the role assigned it from the start. And urban America as much as, if not more than, rural America, in which the myth of Arcadia and utopian communities happily coexisted with the violence of conquest. During the first half of the nineteenth century, Americans regarded the accelerated urbanization underway in a Europe undergoing industrialization as a plague to be avoided, but it wasn't long before a reversal led us to regard the American city, however rigorously gridded it might be, as the crudest expression of "savage" capitalism, and of its crimes as much as its exploits.

Exploits (some would say crimes) of which the skyscraper is not the least remarkable. The skyscraper that has remained profoundly linked to America, in its essence as in its appearance, despite the many attempts to transplant, acclimatize, and hybridize it: in Milan, Paris, Frankfurt, and Tokyo, very tall buildings, even those designed by Americans (like the Tour Montparnasse), are called not skyscrapers but "towers." Doubtless it isn't altogether accurate to say that there are only American skyscrapers (Norman Foster's Hong Kong & Shanghai Bank in Hong Kong proves the contrary); but in a sense there are not, and never can be, any "real" skyscrapers outside of America: Hong Kong being precisely the exception that proves the rule. And one sees perfectly well why: the skyscraper is in no way a type or an autonomous form, any more than it is a model; rather, it is part of an environment in which it can reproduce itself. (Didn't Montaigne's contemporaries worry about their chances of survival if "cannibals" were introduced into Europe?) It found this environment in North America, as well as in Hong Kong, Singapore, and perhaps Caracas and São Paulo. An economic environment, but also and preeminently a landscape, or more accurately an urban site: it's the city that makes the skyscraper, not the skyscraper that makes the city. Chicago, New York, Miami, and even Los Angeles, not to mention cities in Asia and South America, offer proof of this observation, likewise confirmed, *a contrario*, closer to home, by the Défense complex in western Paris. A matter, some would say, of "skyline" as much as of implantation, of elevation rather than ground plan; a matter of *site*, a skyline being all that's needed, when the circumstances are right, to build something completely artificial that nonetheless resembles a landscape—we are right to speak of the "cliffs" of Manhattan—in which skyscrapers can flourish: hence the singular beauty of cities like Hong Kong and Rio de Janeiro, which combine the two aspects, natural and artificial, to spectacular effect. Cities make the skyscraper; but it is architecture (for that is indeed what is in question, as Le Corbusier understood) that makes the site, whether by revealing it or by producing it.

New York is, as Paul Morand maintained, a "horizontal city," and in the highest degree, despite being contained, at least as regards Manhattan, by strict geographic limits. But this, precisely, is one of the reasons European tourists find its image so powerful: Manhattan's boundary is clearly defined and instantly discernible, something that makes it comparable to the fortified cities of old Europe, which could grow only by spreading beyond their successive walls, but sets it apart from other American cities, which have vague boundaries and spread into endless suburbs, the city being distinguishable from its surroundings only by its tighter grid, as in Frank Lloyd Wright's Broadacre City scheme. And this is so despite the exception of San Francisco, whose "European" charm derives as much from the way its architecture produces its site as from the movement imposed on its imperious grid by its rolling hills. But New York also qualifies as a horizontal city because of its skyline, for whenever new vertical structures spring up, at least downtown, it's as though the city were filling gaps in its upper reaches so as to achieve, through a kind of natural process, higher and more continuous facades (the above-mentioned "cliffs").

The European city results, in its form, from what might now be called "integrative urbanism," from operations in which architecture—everything from large buildings to punctuating domes and bell towers—is made to blend into the urban fabric. As to form, the American city is produced merely by distributing the game pieces over a basic checkerboard, an approach that virtually guarantees the predominance of a strictly architectural order: no master plan, no urbanist scheme could assure that the towers erected in the cities of Europe would be sited to such monumental, urban effect as are, at ground level as well as skyline level, the most beautiful skyscrapers in New York and Chicago.

This is, in effect, one of the paradoxes that nourishes "Americanism," at least with regard to architecture. An architecture, let it be said in passing, irreducible to that—the most visible—of the city, an architecture often to be sought elsewhere, in the valleys of Pennsylvania, on the hills of Wisconsin, in remote areas of New England, or hidden by vegetation in the canyons of Pacific Palisades, Bel Air, and Beverly Hills, even in the deepest Arizona desert. I remember Richard Meier's reaction to an article in the *New York Times* in which he was congratulated for never having built a skyscraper: "That's not," he confided to me, "because I didn't want such a commission!" The same Richard Meier whose Atheneum in New Harmony, not far from Kansas City, I had just visited: a visitor's center for the communitarian establishment founded by Robert Owen as phase one of his envisioned utopia: to be sure, its gleaming white concrete bears no traces of the forms from which it was cast, whereas brick prevails over wood in the construction of the houses in the town. And yet, here as there, and in the indefinite extent of the Middle West as in Manhattan's ever-increasing congestion, the image of America derives its strength from the same mythic gesture, although one that goes against the grain of any notion of *foundation* or *origin*.

The European idea of the city is based on the principle of boundaries inscribed on the ground, along the horizontal, whether these are understood to be original, linked to a ritual of foundation, or acknowledged to be the product of necessity, like the fortified walls within which the first human settlements had to be enclosed for reasons of security. When it comes to contours, American cities, Manhattan aside, have only their skylines, which, while inscribed on the vertical, are not, I insist, a matter merely of facade or silhouette. For they proceed, at every moment, in each of their profiles, from what might be called a *pioneer* gesture (here, of course, it is again the myth that speaks): the gesture of the clearers and builders who were the first settlers. Which corresponds quite nicely to the example used by René Thom to illustrate the idea of phenomenological discontinuity: that of a board cut with a saw, along whose edges there is passage from a vertical to a horizontal regimen. The movement of the saw introduced an elementary catastrophe, the static catastrophe with which we must henceforth deal being the result of a dynamic catastrophe that was the board's production.[36] Similarly, the Manhattan skyline can be viewed as a depository of the successive catastrophes that produced it, every one of them provisional, just as the cabins of the first pioneers were infused with memories of the chopping down of the trees and the sawing of the planks from which they were made.

It was not without good reason that Le Corbusier evoked, in connection with New York, the plus sign (+), born of the perpendicular superimposition of two straight lines. The *"signe constructeur,"* as he then called it, which in the present context poses a problem. If America cannot resign itself to the disappearance of the last great sequoias in the Northwest, that is because it sees in them, likewise with good reason, the final stage of clearing, of the "frontier," and at the same time the annunciatory sign of entry into a cycle in which the plays of opposition between vertical and horizontal, dilution and concentration, dissemination and congestion, will no longer obey rules that might be called natural, any more than they will lend themselves to clearly motivated choices. And that regarding, on the level of fantasy, the localization of centers of decision, increasingly less dependent on the concentration of communication networks that led to the vertical city than on images—their correlates—of the state of weightlessness in which the actors of the new "frontier" henceforth evolve, propelled as they themselves are toward the vertical. The scene of life of the future: America is that, like it or not, and perhaps more than ever, to the extent that, on this scene, there are no assured dimensions, just as there are no secure sites, no sets that are not from the start irrevocably dated, just as there is no construction, however one understands the word, and setting aside history and even description, that is not subject to challenge, or at least to constant review as regards its principle, even its definition, narrative as well as structural.

7

Manhattan Transference

What, today, is the place of America, what role can it hence-forth play, in what we generally call an architect's "education," in his or her culture? The question is, of course, no longer as important as it was at the end of the last century, when the young Adolf Loos, leaving his native Vienna for a time, decided to see America for himself; nor does it have the prominence conferred on it, antitheti-cally, by Le Corbusier's belated visit to New York in 1935. None-theless, it retains some meaning, insofar as, through an apt reversal, the same "new world" whose image played, by projection and in fantastic or hallucinatory guise, a determinant role in the crystal-lization and development of the idea of modernity (America, "the scene of life of the future"), this same world (this same America) is presently the scene of a radical questioning of so-called modernist ideology, of which Europe has received—at best—only echoes, and which has found its privileged expression in the field of architectural criticism.

There are many reasons for this, notably the emigration to the United States, on the eve of the Second World War, of many repre-sentatives of the modern movement, among them several masters of the Bauhaus, its preeminent teaching institution: which led to the diffusion, under the influence of the American environment and in response to its specific exigencies, of a singularly reductive and dogmatic version of the modernist program, a trivial, seemingly strictly functional variant that, what's more, was henceforth severed from any activity that might be called "avant-gardist." A matter, we are told, of *translation*, and subject, like the avatars of psychoanalysis in these same years, to an analogous displacement and transference.

Remaining with architecture, it is symptomatic that the reaction prompted, in the United States itself, by the banalization of modernist ideology should have borrowed from the start the means and terminology of the history of styles, whereas the apostles of the modern movement had sought to banish the very notion of style. This regression, clearly calculated, evidences an intention to jettison a tenet that had been central to the "modernist" program: reducing architecture to a matter of style amounts to denying it any value other than the strictly representational or pictorial, whereas the modernist project, as this was constituted during the Enlightenment period, regarded it simultaneously as the instrument of its realization and as the proof (or sign) of its having been achieved. The world, society, the entire edifice of human institutions was posited as something *to be built*, and the resulting structures were to be monumental: either revolution was considered a necessary precondition for solving the "housing problem" (architecture *and* revolution), or architecture was regarded, precisely, as a means of avoiding revolution (architecture *or* revolution)—when, that is, one didn't follow the same path as the Russian constructivists and regard architecture as a servant of revolution.

Jefferson's America took up this project but on its own terms, those of a society that was essentially agrarian and profoundly opposed to the idea of the "metropolis"—in every sense of the word, whether in the form of the colonialist yoke from which it had to free itself by means of a movement that it itself described as revolutionary, or in that of the great urban agglomerations in Europe, horrific spectacles that were then taking shape as a result of rapid industrialization. When this evil began to make inroads in the United States,

there seemed to be a radical divergence between the supporters of an
antiurban ideology and the men in Chicago and New York—promoters, engineers, architects—who saw themselves as the fabrica-
tors of a new culture. On one hand, adepts of the Prairie School
who, under the leadership of Frank Lloyd Wright, maintained that
the only viable response to population growth and increasing urban
density was the transformation of America into a gigantic suburb,
Wright's Broadacre City; on the other hand, the skyscraper builders,
the constructors of what Le Corbusier described as "titanic miner-
ologies" whose "violent silhouettes" resembled giant "fever charts"
rising alongside the waterways of the Loop and on the bedrock of
Manhattan[1]—the problem being (insofar as this caricatural characterization of the opposition is tenable) that of determining which of
the two sides was that of "modernity." But the degree to which European architects emigrating to the United States were amenable to
compromise indicates that the real question lay elsewhere, that it
had less to do with form and style than with the ways that modernity could manifest itself in either context.

　　To return to the nature of America's present role in an architect's training and culture: it is clear that the application of the question is not limited to European architects, to say nothing of those in
Japan, China, South America, and so forth. I have evoked some of
the factors underlying the fact that the debate—or supposed debate
—over modernity was born in America, and preeminently in the
field of architecture. But if it is true that this debate is especially pertinent to the American context, if it is true that, within this context,
it is linked, paradoxically, to modernity in its most universal aspect
and thus might help us to formulate the question better and to determine its real stakes, then America's status as the chosen land of
this question becomes a matter of considerable importance for anyone with an artistic calling, whatever their situation in relation to the
Atlantic or the Pacific, beginning with those who are just beginning
their careers. And the remark applies to American architects themselves. Determining whether or not one is, or aspires to be, an American is not necessarily a simple matter—especially for artists and ar-

chitects, who participate as such, willingly or otherwise, in a history that is not confined to America, and in which the latter's place is anything but predetermined. Having been prepared, notably, by the Museum of Modern Art in New York, by men like Alfred Barr and even Philip Johnson (who has now embraced the cause of "post-modernism"), the arrival in the United States toward the end of the 1930s of a considerable number of European architects and, a bit later, artists, and the corollary translation of modernist ideology into the vernacular, did not suffice to make American artists and architects more fully cognizant of their own *position*. Such a shift in consciousness would be effected only when the distance—distance from Europe, but also distance from the specifically American context—constituting the singularity of this situation, of this position, was transformed, and, in a characteristic involution, there was a reversal of the signs for exterior and interior, for the foreign (read: exotic) and the indigenous or familiar, always threatened with turning into its opposite, the disquieting, the unfamiliar, the *unheimlich* (uncanny). The reaction against the trivial, banalized version of modernist ideology that has prevailed in the United States has not failed to accrue there "European" connotations which, at first glance, seem paradoxical, given that the ideology itself was an import. But the fact that the graft took so easily, and to such striking effect, should have prompted some of the leading critical minds of the American architectural world to ask questions about the eminently complex and even contradictory nature of the relations the country has maintained (and continues to maintain, if only after the fact) with "modernism," however one understands this word—but that, precisely, is part of the question.

Let us now consider an apprentice from the Old World who chose, from the start, to associate the practice of architecture with a kind of geographical roaming that borders on schizophrenia, although it is entirely deliberate and controlled: a story or a history (*histoire*: more than theory is in question) of permanently exposing his professional life to this same power of transference that displaced the question of modernism, historically speaking, from Europe to

America, with the effects noted above. The said apprentice, who left
Holland quite early and spent four years at the Architectural Association School (AAS) in London shortly after 1968, would soon arrive
in the United States with the idea already in his head of producing a
piece of work about New York. But what kind of work, and why
about New York? If the point of departure (Holland) was not in-
consequential, this is not only because the first Europeans to establish themselves on the island of Manhattan were Dutch, and because
they immediately set about reconstituting a bit of their mother
country on this untamed land, to the point of excavating out of the
rock a canal that was soon lined by gabled houses. As is well known,
Holland is not exclusively a land of nostalgia: from Berlage to Riet-
veld, Oud, and Bakema, from Van Doesburg to Mondrian, it has
mobilized warriors in a fight for "modernism," often programmatic
in character, that encountered concerted resistance on both political
and institutional fronts—resistance that is still present, still active.

Rem Koolhaas would gain harsh experience of this resistance
after returning to his country. But in his case, can we really speak of
a *return*, given that the constant aerial peregrinations that regularly
take the architect to America have never ceased—as though he felt
compelled to repeat the movement that initially led him there? If
Rem Koolhaas has learned anything from his transatlantic flights
and from his "work" on New York, it is that the conditions of avant-
garde practice (if this phrase still means anything) as well as the
forms issuing from it have changed radically since the period of the
"historical" avant-gardes: to such an extent that today it is difficult
to conceive of the possibility of any such practice, or to acknowledge
its necessity, with the result that we are apt to view any and all attempts to renew with "avant-garde" language and practice as co-
medic exercises in which nostalgia vies with a rhetoric that is strictly
repetitive, like that, on occasion, of the unconscious. There is nothing about this rapprochement that would upset Rem Koolhaas. But
if he has not renounced the idea of avant-garde activity, at least in
the field of architecture—let me rephrase: if he lays claim to this
designation for his own work, that is because he has managed to for-

mulate, in the clearest possible terms, an idea of what such activity presently entails, and of what its viable field of application and points of maximum impact might be. In other words, he is one of very few today who can legitimately claim to possess both a project and a theory, a strategy and an ethic: the problem being to understand properly that this project and this theory, this strategy and this ethic, are indissociable from both the power of displacement and the above-mentioned effects of transference. Further: that the latter are the very conditions of their existence, circumstances on which they are entirely dependent. Assuming there can and should be avant-garde work today, such work cannot take (a) place [*avoir (de) lieu*], whereas the historical avant-gardes were situated in their time, each in its own way, in specific contexts. It must be everywhere and nowhere (which is not the same as ascribing to it a "global" dimension), and it must achieve this by means of a distancing (and a suspension) whose literal metaphor is air travel.

In fact, the "historical" avant-gardes themselves were constituted, became established, gained recognition only at the price, already, of displacements and transferences of one kind or another. The first manifesto of Italian Futurism was published in Paris, in *Le Figaro*; Theo Van Doesburg's professional travels are well known; and the meeting in Berlin, in 1923, of the Soviet artist El Lissitzky and the German architect Mies Van der Rohe can be taken as emblematic of the birth of an international, even internationalist, avant-garde (Lissitzky's "isms"). In the same sense, it is said over and over that America, which was still provincial as regards the visual arts, acquired an avant-garde only by proxy, and by way of individuals who were themselves "displaced" in various respects, for example, Gertrude Stein and Ezra Pound. Hence—*this* explains *that*—the nostalgic bent of some American architects today, who are said to recycle, more or less consciously, more or less cynically, formulas introduced by the avant-garde of the 1920s, in the process adapting them to contemporary taste and rendering them acceptable to an American public. This assessment would be valid only if America had never known an avant-garde. But Rem Koolhaas, to his considerable credit, has demonstrated, by means of his gift for historical analysis (in its way, *Delirious New York*[2] is a great work of history, one worthy of comparison with Walter Benjamin's *Arcades Project*), that Manhattan, between 1890 and 1940, was a center of work that might well be called avant-garde, but that had to realize itself by means other than those open to the European avant-gardes: beginning with the fact that this work involved neither an organized, self-conscious avant-garde movement nor the publication of collective manifestos. Better (or worse) still: it was able to develop and produce its effects only insofar as the theory from which it issued remained unformulated, if not unconscious.

It is this theory that Rem Koolhaas set out to reveal, at the same time that he added a new term to the catalogue of "isms" deemed to correspond to the different movements that establish the rhythm specific to the history of modern art. But "Manhattanism" is unique in that, unlike many manifestos that remained a dead letter, its realization was dependent upon a renunciation of all explicit enunciation, and many of its implementers went so far as to make statements directly at odds with their actual practice. This divergence, this radical discrepancy between avowed intentions and real aims, was more than the consistent mainspring of the development of Manhattan; according to Koolhaas, it is the key to what by rights must be designated *the strategy of its realization*.

If this has passed unnoticed, that is because this strategy, this program, this theory, insofar as it remained implicit (the growth of New York, like that of Chicago, resembling in many respects a natural process, even a natural cataclysm), ran directly counter to what was to become an article of Modernist dogma. "It is a catastrophe," Le Corbusier said upon arriving in New York—adding immediately: "but a beautiful and worthy catastrophe."[3] As if "the ecstasy before architecture" (Koolhaas's phrase) that everyone—independent of all considerations of taste, ideology, and fashion—experiences in New York (as in Chicago), as if the fascination of this "stupefying city" had proved irresistible to the apostle of the Radiant City without making him forget his own dogma, according to which there could be no new architecture without a new urbanism. "Radiant," Manhattan certainly was not that, at least not in Le Corbusier's sense, for it did not conform to the rules for which he had propagandized throughout the world. But beautiful, certainly, and magical, although he regarded the *wildness* of its beauty and magic as an invitation to recast it, to rebuild it completely and make of it, in his words, "something grander still, but under control."

When Le Corbusier discovered America, he immediately took up the discourse of those who had been the first to arrive: the same principles that Rem Koolhaas—citing a book on New York published in 1849—described as *exterminators*, and that were supposed to result in the systematic elimination of the "savagery" (another word for "barbarism") and its replacement by forms of life that were more refined, more "civilized." But, as is well known, the positions of savagery and civilization are reversible: one is always another's barbarian, if not one's own. The same Le Corbusier would not hesitate to describe New York as a "savage city," despite his admiration for its cleanliness, its brilliance, its diamantine sparkle.

Good God, what disorder, what impetuosity! What perfection already, what promises! What unity in a molecular state, gridiron street plan, office on top of office, clear crystallization. It is sublime and atrocious, but nothing works any more. There is nothing for it but to see clearly, to think, to conceive, to start over.

And the passage, whose peremptory tone is altogether characteristic, concludes in the first person—so true is it that the only way to be done with savagery is to exterminate the savages, to clear the way such that one can occupy the terrain oneself and take things in hand: "Yes, I was mistaken. Let's start over!"

The Americans did not wait for Le Corbusier to make a fresh start. In the "theater of progress" that is Manhattan (but if it is a theater, then where, precisely, is its stage?),

the performance can never end or even progress, in the conventional sense of dramatic plotting; it can only be the cyclic restatement of a single theme: creation and destruction irrevocably interlocked, endlessly reenacted.

The exterminating principles remain forever active; "what is refinement one moment will be barbarism the next."[4] What's more, these principles could operate only within a specific framework—strictly determined, regulated, controlled—consistent with the imperious street grid imposed on much of Manhattan by the plan of 1811, when most of the island was as yet unoccupied: an organizational scheme traditionally associated with colonial settlements but here implemented on a scale so large as to be almost fantastic, the city's growth acquiring from that moment the appearance of an infinitely renewed experiment with limits.

It would be impossible to find a better illustration of this than the genealogy of the New York skyscraper as sketched by Rem Koolhaas, issuing as it did (the skyscraper) from the "fortuitous encounter," within the above-mentioned matrix, of three distinct urbanist innovations: the proliferation of superimposed platforms, made possible by technological advances; the tower, a symbol of technological progress as well as—of necessity, given its lofty autonomy—a figure of defiance; and, finally, the "block" whose four defining streets determine, a priori, the limit of all architectural intention as well as of all urbanist enterprise. A limit operative at ground level, if we remain with the philosophy implicit in the grid and its inscription on a two-dimensional plane; but a limit, also, in terms of volume and even height, from the moment it became clear that this philosophy entailed a real corrective: the process of territorial reproduction (the multiplication, pure and simple, of the block) could only lead to chaos, as a result of a kind of natural selection in which individual success was measured in terms of the destruction of adjacent structures. The zoning law of 1916 put an end to what Rem Koolhaas aptly calls "architectural murder" by stipulating for each block in Manhattan "an imaginary envelope that defines the outlines of the maximum allowable construction."[5] For, despite its being applicable only within individual blocks, the law nonetheless regulated the "final and conclusive" occupancy of Manhattan, defining it as a *"Mega-Village"* consisting of—according to the basic grid, which was accepted as a given—2,028 "colossal phantom 'houses'" defined by thirteen streets running north-south and 156 crosstown streets (13 x 156). All that remained was for a "delineator" like Hugh Ferris to complete the process initiated with the 1811 plan by executing charcoal drawings of the fantastic masses, stripped of all superfluous detail as well as of all the stigmatas of eclecticism, that would be those of "the metropolis of tomorrow"—the title of the book Ferris published in 1929, the year of the stock-market crash.[6]

The 1916 law was meant to preclude abuses not prevented by the imposition of the street grid, which the authors of the 1811 plan had explicitly conceived to this end: excesses that, despite the containing element of the block system, resembled a natural catastrophe. The widespread view that architects in New York and Chicago were the often unknowing instruments of a growth that eluded their control and whose implications they frequently underestimated, this view seems to be confirmed by the fact that, when the moment arrived for them to reflect on the new forms of urban development, they only embraced with intensified ardor the development that had pushed the city upward: they declared the skyscraper to be "inevitable," maintaining that the best one could do would be to adapt such structures by building ever higher, but in such a way that larger areas at ground level would be left open, thereby improving the circulation of light and air as well as ameliorating traffic congestion. Harvey Wiley Corbett's image of a "modernized Venice" in which automobile and pedestrian traffic would be separated from one another thanks to the construction of shopping arcades above street level linked by a network of pedestrian bridges, an image, whose utopian force derives from the metaphorical transference that is its justification, reveals the ambivalence inherent in the position adopted by theorists of the skyscraper:

Theory, if there is to be any, will be adapted to the Skyscraper, not the Skyscraper to the theory. . . . To secure the Skyscraper's continuing license to create congestion, they embark, ostensibly, on a crusade of *decongestion*.[7]

Le Corbusier said much the same thing: "The skyscrapers are too small!" (even as he pronounced them greater, *in terms of style,* than their architects). But his assertion was unequivocal. What he admired about American skyscrapers was the evidence they provided of the new dimensions—in terms of both breadth and height—now available to architecture, and of the technological developments that made them possible. Beginning with elevators able to whisk you to the sixty-fifth floor, without mishap, in about as much time as it took, in Paris, to climb to the sixth floor—with this corollary, so revealing of the different nature of the two types of urban dynamic: in Europe, elevators were introduced into apartment buildings in the finer neighborhoods so that the privileged could reside on upper floors hitherto reserved for servants, whereas in Manhattan the same invention (initially introduced to the public at the 1853 world's fair) facilitated a radical diversification of all aspects of the urban scene, in ways inconceivable in the Old World.

Now it is precisely this that the purportedly unconscious adepts of Manhattanism were not prepared to renounce. (Note that calling these adepts "unconscious" is not the same thing as reducing them to the mere passive agents of capital in its speculative and bureaucratic guises.) Le Corbusier maintained that the formidable concentration of human beings made possible by skyscrapers could facilitate a considerable reduction in surface construction—if, that is, these tall buildings were widely spaced.[8] For he saw skyscrapers, however "Cartesian" they might be, as mere tools intended to serve specific functions that were primarily bureaucratic in nature ("In Algiers, a single skyscraper will suffice. In Barcelona, two skyscrapers. In Antwerp, three skyscrapers. . . . Business communities will be vertical, set in the midst of immense green parks"). But the skyscrapers in Manhattan were quite different (Le Corbusier neither could nor would see this, just as theorists of the skyscraper neither could nor would *say* it). The Manhattan of Manhattanism was not merely a business community; it was also the site of encounters and pleasures of which skyscrapers presented competing views, offering its inhabitants the spectacle, inscribed in stone, concrete, and steel, of a way of life obeying a very different program, one answering a question quite different from that of "housing." In the shift from one scene to another (from one modernity to another; but then they are all of a piece), the point of view changed radically: in the Radiant City, everyone was to have at his disposal a domicile supplied with sun and light as well as with a view stretching toward the horizon; from skyscraper heights (as already from the top of the Eiffel Tower, but in a different context), the metropolis multiplied, for the benefit of those present there only as spectators (as still, in Paris or New York, when one crosses or stations oneself on a bridge[9]), the plunging views of the city and the promises of pleasure of all kinds that it harbors in its depths, as on each of its floors, being multiplied indefinitely.

There is no better illustration of the difference between these two versions of modernity—the one rejecting the very notion of the "metropolis," the other embracing it to excess—than the "overhead views" made possible by lofty buildings and airplanes (as well as, today, by helicopters): so prominent a representative of modernist ideology as Walter Gropius, the founder of the Bauhaus, who emigrated to the United States in 1936, claimed that one of the advantages of flat, terraced roofs was that they would make cities virtually indiscernible from the air, leaving visible only structures drowning in greenery.[10] In the matter of greenery, Manhattan would content itself with the large but strictly delimited, hundred-and-fifty-three block area of Central Park, now surrounded by tall residential buildings, the oldest of which culminate in pyramids or spires pointing heavenwards. But this park, created in the mid-nineteenth century, was intended less to inscribe the future city within a natural framework, in a way consistent with the ideology of the Radiant City, than to preserve in the island's center a sample of nature that would make it possible to measure, by comparison, the evolution of the site in the context of the metropolis to come: "a taxidermic preservation of nature that exhibits forever the drama of culture outdistancing nature,"[11] like the great national parks, first envisioned in this same period; a drama likewise central to the conquest of the West and to the myth of the "frontier"—a myth to which skyscrapers contributed in their fashion by testing the limits of vertical expansion. With the caveat that Olmstead's Central Park was the product of manipulations more visible than those effected at Yellowstone and Yosemite. "A synthetic Arcadian carpet": such is Rem Koolhaas's characterization of Central Park, whose modest, late-twentieth-century equivalent is a relatively small fenced plot, situated on La Guardia Place between Houston and Bleeker streets, that purports to offer passers-by a sample of the flora of Manhattan prior to the arrival of Europeans.

It is as though the creators of Central Park had foreseen the specifics of the future metropolitan condition: the obliteration of nature, and the triumph of artifice to the point of fantasy, under the double effect of density and of a culture that would use all of its technological resources to play, by design, the card of *congestion*. Again, none of these things could be explicitly articulated. Let us repeat, with Rem Koolhaas: the program of Manhattanism managed to impose itself, to become reality, only insofar as it remained unformulated, only to the extent that theorists of the day spoke the ostensibly "modernist" language of decongestion so as to improve the chances of the skyscraper. The architect who most fully embodied the spirit of Manhattanism, Raymond Hood, long kept secret his vision of the Manhattan of the future as a City of (independent and rival) Towers, before publishing—again, the very year of the Wall Street crash—a project for a City under a Single Roof which posited that the only solution to the problem of congestion created by skyscrapers was the constitution of enormous, interdependent complexes each of which would contain entire branches of industry, clubs, hotels, shops, apartments, and even theaters, thereby minimizing the need for horizontal displacement at ground level, replacing this with vertical movement inside these large structures.

Rockefeller Center (of which Hood was one of the principal fashioners) is

the most mature demonstration of Manhattanism's unspoken theory of the simultaneous existence of different programs on a single site, connected only by the common data of elevators, service cores, columns and external envelope.[12]

But this theory was first implemented in 1931, in the Downtown Athletic Club, whose thirty-eight superimposed floors offered metropolitan bachelors a full array of sports facilities, artificial landscapes, social spaces, and bedrooms, all linked by elevators: "machine[s] fostering and intensifying the most desirable modes of human contact" answering in every particular, in a different political and cultural context, to the notion of the skyscraper as "social condenser" introduced in 1926 by Alexander Pasternak (Boris's brother), even as they reproduced, on each floor, at each strata, a fragmentary "montage of attractions" (in Eisenstein's sense) that are the principal asset of metropolitan life but that elude all efforts to control them. It is often said that America has no monuments; indeed, the skyscraper belongs to a new category: that of the Automonument, a structure referencing only itself but that, given its considerable volume, cannot avoid becoming an empty symbol, one open to all manner of signification, to "plots" and "stories" of every stripe.

Displacement and condensation: it is not a matter of chance that these two terms correspond to the two operations characteristic of unconscious processes, and principally of dreams. In his work on New York, Rem Koolhaas has isolated something that resembles an amnesia, in the psychoanalytic sense of the word. And how could it have been otherwise, given that he effectively set himself the task of translating into words an unformulated, even unconscious program whose visible manifestation is the Manhattan skyline? *Architects have a right to the unconscious*: this statement holds for the analyst as well as for the analysand, and without its always being clear who or which is the other's plaything: the architect, whose inner life is subject to manipulation by the unconscious of his or her culture; or the unconscious itself, which the analyst delights in trying to outwit, in the rather mad hope of beating it at its own game.

A game inextricable from those played by memory. If it is true that nothing in psychic life is ever lost, that everything it registers is retained, one way or another, such that it can resurface, then what might we learn, asked Freud, by comparing this psychic life with what archaeology reveals to us about the past of a city— beginning (as one must) with the city rightly called "eternal," to which he constantly refers in his oeuvre? As Freud himself observed, if everything were retained from all the successive periods of Roman history, the results would be absurd: on the present site of the Pantheon, we would find not only the building of Augustus but also that of Agrippa; and the same plot of ground would support both the Church of Santa Maria Sopra Minerva and the ancient temple that it replaced in the Middle Ages. So the analogy is not complete. Even so, Freud clearly was not prepared to renounce it, if only (he maintained) because it showed "how far we are from mastering the characteristics of mental life by representing them in pictorial terms."[13] But why did he find it necessary to evoke visual images, figuration, in this connection if not because the mind itself must, at one time or another, have passed the same way, have found its *place* in them?

The archaeological metaphor is problematic, Freud also says, in that the hypothesis of an integral conservation of the past is applicable to mental life only if the psychic organ remains intact, whereas a city's development entails deliberate demolitions, which might themselves be analogous to morbid phenomena. For, as we have already seen, nothing precludes a reversal of the terms of the comparison, or use of the psychic metaphor to clarify, with the aid of images borrowed from mental life, certain turns and evasions of urban memory—and, even more, of metropolitan memory. We know that a catastrophe can occasion the reconstruction on different sites of buildings that were obliged, in the course of history, to cede their place to other building (as in the reconstruction of Warsaw after World War II). But such is also the case, a fortiori, for the "capital of perpetual crisis" (disruptive episodes that are now replacing revolution as the mainsprings and permanent horizons of history) that is Manhattan: Manhattan, whose development is the very image of the operations—displacement, condensation—of the unconscious. Without taking into account that at least one thing remains intact throughout the metropolis' history: the grid, which has never been challenged or altered (the only permissible deviations being the rounding of the corners of blocks or their perforation, of which there are all too many examples today), and which has functioned from the start as a memory template of unmatched rigor.

In effect, this template dictated that the architectural components of all "urbanist" operations be contained within the limits of a single block (Hood's "Manhattan 1950" project, which called for the construction of thirty-eight "mountains" at important intersections of the grid, reveals how constraining it was). This incontrovertible rule had many consequences, some of them real, even material, and others in the order of the imaginary, even of fantasy, when they did not lend themselves to symbolic development, linked as they both were to effects of condensation as well as to the displacements entailed by the block system. Rem Koolhaas has shown how Coney Island's successful "montage of attractions" served as an incubator for the mythology and the thematics that were to be those of Manhattanism, the amusement park constituting a test run for a true "technology of fantasy." But this technology would be able to produce all of its fruit only after being transferred to the island of Manhattan and subjected to the dominion of the grid that this entailed.

Such a transfer did not entail the substitution of reality for fantasy. Rather, it was fantasy that, accruing the form and coherence of architecture, began to seem like reality. When, upon returning to New York after spending more than three decades in Europe, the protagonist of Henry James's "The Jolly Corner" tries to assess "the differences, the newnesses, the queernesses, above all the bignesses" that "assaulted his vision wherever he looked," he soon becomes anxious about the "ghosts" that would surely disturb the conversion of the house in which he had been born into a skyscraper. Without doubt, as a friend points out to him, he could well afford to be sentimental about the operation, given the profit he would reap from it. But in fact, the transformations of Manhattan seem to have obeyed, from the start, the rule of mental life stipulating the retention of everything in every successive evolutionary phase, such that the past can always return in one form or another when the occasion presents itself.

Here again, something one might be tempted to regard as a natural phenomenon has every appearance of being the result of deliberate intention. When, on the orders of William Waldorf Astor, his commodious family residence, on a site formerly occupied by a farm, was in its turn replaced by a hotel, the architects were instructed to preserve as much of the *aura* of the place as possible:

For Astor, the destruction of a structure does not preclude the preservation of its spirit; with his Waldorf he injects the concept of reincarnation into architecture. . . . The transplantations from the Astor mansions—literal or merely by nomenclature—suggest that the Waldorf-Astoria is conceived by its promoters as a haunted house, rife with the ghosts of its predecessors. To construct a House haunted by its own past and those of other buildings: such is the Manhattanist strategy for the production of vicarious history.[14]

But before long, the block's value had so greatly increased that it became imperative to destroy the first hotel to make way for a skyscraper that would surpass all of its competitors in both size and beauty. The idea of the Waldorf (a "residential complex" suited to the exigencies of modern life) would resurface, through displacement, at another point on the grid, while the Empire State Building, which recycled certain elements of the earlier building (beginning with its elevator cores), rose on the same plot, exemplifying a form of architectural cannibalism in which the final building absorbs the power of the site's previous occupants and perpetuates their memory. "The *Empire State Building* is . . . the climax of the subconscious Manhattan. The *Waldorf* is the first full realization of the conscious Manhattan."[15] But both saw light of day only to mimic, to the point of seeming to give them a proper history, the processes of the unconscious.

Delirious New York was written by a young architect at the beginning of his career, and it has all the characteristics of a bildungsroman, a novel of apprenticeship or education: as often in such texts, the experience he relates is that of a conversion that could just as well have been its mainspring as its result. In effect, the young Rem Koolhaas knew perfectly well what he would look for in New York, and what the consequences of such a transfer would be for him, as well as what work of anamnesis such a move would occasion for him: in the end, this novel about the formation of an architect is indistinguishable from that of the metropolis itself. Manhattan, capital of the twentieth century, and of a twentieth century that is now drawing to a close, in much the same way that Walter Benjamin took Paris to be the capital of the nineteenth century? If Rem Koolhaas set out to write the *retrospective* manifesto of Manhattan (and of Manhattanism), this was not only as a historian, with retrospective ends but also with critical and even polemical ones: for him, it was a question of preventing a part of twentieth-century culture, one that had lost none of its currency, from falling into an oblivion to which the debate over modernism threatened to relegate it:

Manhattanism is the one urbanistic ideology that has fed, from its conception, on the splendors and miseries of the metropolitan condition—hyperdensity—without once losing faith in it as the basis for a desirable modern culture. . . . The retroactive formulation of Manhattan's program is a polemical operation. It reveals a number of theorems and breakthroughs that not only give logic and pattern to the city's past performance, but whose containing validity is itself an argument for a second coming of Manhattanism, this time as an explicit doctrine that can transcend the island of its origins to claim a place among contemporary urbanisms.[16]

This book, which proposes, through the image of Manhattan, "a blueprint for a Culture of Congestion," was, then, the fruit of specifically psychoanalytic work. A work of memory as much as of rendering explicit (the aspects being mutually inextricable), and one aiming to (re)establish the architect as the subject of a history of which he had been dispossessed as the result of a repression whose object was a part of the culture of modernity. To regard movies as the preeminent art form of the twentieth century (with architecture, its only *living* art, declared Erwin Panofsky in 1933, shortly after disembarking in New York[17]) does not necessarily entail dismissal of painting or the performing arts, any more than the recent appearance of digital imaging signifies that we have entered a "postcine-matic" age. The problem is, rather, to take the measure, in each case, of the repression that is one of the mainsprings of this ceaseless for-ward impetus, and of the losses it entails in terms of historical expe-rience. The same applies to that *other* culture of modernity (or to that culture of *another* modernity) for which Manhattan was simul-taneously the laboratory and the set shop, but whose lesson we pre-fer to forget today, retaining only its picturesque aspects. If Rem Koolhaas obstinately denounces the fatalist notion that each genera-tion must reject the heritage of the preceding one, if he himself lays claim to the last of the great Manhattan architects (including Wal-lace K. Harrison, who gave concrete form to Le Corbusier's theoret-ical proposal for the United Nations headquarters), it is for reasons that have nothing to do with nostalgia, reasons that, in the present context, are strategic in character. At a moment when architectural discourse has been reduced to a matter of style, and when commis-sioning institutions assess designs primarily in terms of their adver-tising and public-relations value, surely it is symptomatic that it has been left to an architect to defend, against all and sundry, the emi-nently "modern" notion of the *program*, by opposing to the cult of signs and simulacra the reality of the unconscious processes that gave the project for a "metropolitan culture" a specifically libidinal charge.

8

Memory Trouble at the Movies

For Gilles Deleuze

Not far off, Manhattan, whose skyline serves as backdrop for the movements of Fred Astaire and Gene Kelly: I had no difficulty making the choice—one that will be regarded, I fear, as incorrigibly frivolous. Reflecting on a challenge I had set myself, namely to write, on the eve of the centenary of motion pictures, a few pages, again as an exercise, about one of my favorite films, a single title immediately sprang to mind: *The Bandwagon* by Vincente Minnelli. For one thing, the title under which it was released in France—*Tous en scène* (Everybody on stage)—explicitly emphasizes the idea of the "scene" or "set," a preoccupation of these exercises. Perhaps more important, this film has remained vivid in my memory ever since the day, long ago, when I first saw it. And this for reasons that I thought were quite clear, as they seemed, essentially, to be a matter of *pleasure*: a pleasure that was renewed every time I saw the film again, or had occasion to talk about it with friends who, like myself, loved jazz (which might seem surprising, given the contempt with which self-appointed guardians of the temple often regard the Broadway theater, and the music of Gershwin and Cole Porter). To talk about it, or rather to rekindle together memories of various episodes and scenes, various dance or ballet sequences, even songs evoked in turn by memorable recordings (Tal Farlow's version of "You and the Night and the Music," renditions of "Dancing in the Dark" by Ella Fitzgerald and—why not, given that the film's appeal derives from its unabashed celebration of entertainment, of spectacle?—Frank Sinatra). Until the day when, reading *Cinema 2: The Time-Image* by Gilles Deleuze, I was startled and gratified to discover (not without a twinge of jealousy) that this wide-ranging philosopher had managed to use musical comedy to explain Henri Bergson, showing how, in Minnelli's work, the genre approaches the mystery of memory, of dream and time, as well as a point where the real and the imaginary become mutually indistinguishable.[1] Whereas I, for my part, could only mimic repeatedly, in thought, word, and gesture, with the delectation that accompanies memories of *jouissance*, the subtle transitions from walking to dancing—or, as Deleuze puts it, from motor steps to dance steps—that are recurrent and constitutive features of the pas de deux (rarely has the phrase been so apt) performed by Fred Astaire and his various partners, and that attain their apogee in his dances with Cyd Charisse.

If *The Bandwagon* struck me as the inevitable choice for my present purposes, this was not only, nor even primarily, because of the mix of more or less equivocal reasons evoked above (no judgments of taste are more *disinterested*, in the Kantian sense, more intimately linked to the sphere and secret history of desire, than the ones we make about movies, and especially about musical comedies, a hybrid genre that nonetheless has sustained a privileged relation—this is a critical commonplace—to the very "essence" of cinema). My real reasons were more obscure. A few days earlier, I had made a mistake of a kind now familiar to movie-lovers who own VCRs. As the no longer extant "Ciné-club" on France 2 (whose sole function was to perpetuate the fiction that television is a daughter of film by paying homage to it, whereas in fact television usually made do with shamelessly exploiting it) had programmed several musical comedies produced by the Arthur Freed unit at Metro-Goldwyn-Mayer, I prepared to record *The Bandwagon*, just as I had recorded *Singin' in the Rain* the week before. Especially given that the broadcast was to include, as an added attraction, a dance number entitled (perhaps in homage to Lubitsch and Greta Garbo) "Two-Faced Woman," a sequence cut from the version of the film that was released but whose absence is perhaps indicated there by a gap in the numbering in the printed program, shots of which are used as segues to various numbers being tried out on the road: the big closing extravaganza, "The Girl Hunt," having been withheld from our view until the New York opening. A well-worn conceit, but one here given a new twist by the presentation of four more stage numbers in rapid-fire succession, each of them being preceded, without any letup in the rhythm, by the shot of a streamlined train speeding, alternatively, toward the viewer's right or left, and headed toward a city whose name is superimposed (Boston, Washington, Baltimore, Philadelphia)—until the same train is shown, moving more slowly and away from the viewer, entering a tunnel just before arriving at Pennsylvania Station, which is not far from the theater where the show that gives the movie its title—*The Bandwagon*—is about to open on Broadway.

If there is any question of a mistake here, it amounts to my having forgotten to set the VCR to channel 2, with the result that, instead of *The Bandwagon*, it recorded, to my considerable irritation, an especially wretched program. But in this instance, it would be better to speak not of a mistake but of memory trouble. Of a muddled memory, or rather of its echo, its index, its fallout, insofar as the disappointment that I experienced while watching the actual broadcast was not only the result of the diminutive size of Minnelli's images on the small screen (in fact, it seemed to me that, paradoxically, the Faustian scene built around "You and the Night and the Music," in which a rehearsal is cut short because smoke from multiple explosions and garishly colored lights suffocate the dancers, physically as well as chromatically, worked quite well on television). More humiliating for me was the discovery that my memory had utterly disfigured the key sequence: whereas in the film we do not see Hunter and Gabrielle descend from the hansom that has brought them to Central Park, and to which they return at the end of the sequence, easing into it without a word but still holding hands, as serene as if they had just made love, I cherished in memory the image—still pristine after my reading of Deleuze—of a descent from the hansom by night, very slow and supple, and of a gradual transition, from that moment, into the actual dance. For I had forgotten the still-tense couple's intervening stroll through an open-air dance, their feigned relaxation as they silently prepare for the ordeal ("Can we dance together?"), until they reach a site where it can take place: a scene secluded and sunken, almost a hollow, as indicated by the few steps that they slowly descend shortly after arriving in the park, and that they later ascend while dancing.

My own personal memory trouble, then. But also a troubling of the innate, congenital memory of cinema itself. Or, more precisely, a troubling of the kind of memory fostered by the movies, that on which they work, that which is their precondition, on which their use, indeed their very production, depends, and whose operation is threatened by the advent of video, and in several ways. To be sure, from the beginning, the number of copies of any given film could be multiplied (an effect of what Benjamin called "technical reproducibility"), and they could be shown at will, given access to the necessary equipment. But this same cinema that Benjamin regarded as the contemporary art form in which the role of the *aura* was most attenuated, because of its having replaced the *hic et nunc* of the traditional work of art, the individual vision, with ubiquitous, infinitely repeatable mass entertainments, this cinema, for all that, is not devoid of cultural value, nor has it completely renounced the search for authenticity. From the cult of the actor (evoked ironically in *The Bandwagon*) to the "auteur theory" (Minnelli being one of the auteurs in question), from the proliferation of revival houses to the preparation of "new" prints, restored with all the care that today's specialists can muster (a case in point being *The Bandwagon*, a cult film if ever there was one), the same desire manifests itself—one distinctly at odds with the demands that movies initially placed upon us. For, however faulty or mistaken might be the memories we took away from our first viewing of a film, it was understood that

they would retain all of their value and pertinence: so many indica-
tions—especially given the resistance and the work of fantasy evidenced by them—of the irreducible impact that a film can have on
a viewer who is seeing it for the first time.

The impact of a film, and not of its copy in video, insofar as
the latter—aside from the fact that such copies are not identical reproductions—entails, as a result of its ready accessibility in cassette
form, a profound alteration of the viewer's relation to film. Benjamin rightly noted that films require a more sustained kind of attention than do paintings. Paintings invite contemplation but allow the
viewer full latitude to surrender, in their presence, to the association
of ideas; whereas at the movies, the eye is transformed virtually from
the moment it first grasps an image.[3] The reader of a book is perfectly free to stop reading, for example to backtrack in order to clarify a point that seems obscure, but the same does not hold for a
movie, which no more welcomes attention lapses than it does sleep,
however frequent these might be: which doesn't prevent *distraction*
—escape, a flight outside of oneself still more radical than Hollywood's version of the Pascalian diversion, than *entertainment* of the
kind so vocally celebrated by the cast of *The Bandwagon*—from being, in this instance, a precondition of reception.

In *America the Menace: Scenes from the Life of the Future*,
Georges Duhamel (whom Benjamin cites) noted that, at the movies,
"My thoughts were no longer under my own control. The moving
pictures usurped the place of my own ideas."[4] But isn't this also true,
in varying degrees, of theatrical performances of all kinds, save that
the movement whereby one participates vicariously in them through
a kind of blind recognition, a movement that Merleau-Ponty deemed
"irreducible,"[5] cannot seem as free in a movie theater as it does at the
opera or the theater? The difference between them residing less in the
relative darkness of the hall than in the very substance of what is seen
and heard there, which at the movies, through the intermediary of a
luminous projection on a screen, is a substitute for the psychic projection elicited by the theatrical setup. For movies, with their talk and
their singing (beginning with *The Jazz Singer*), sometimes comple-

mented by dancing to the accompaniment of music of different kinds (as Patrick Brion has noted, "talking pictures" issued, in part, from a desire to do cinematic justice to the magnificence of Broadway productions, beginning with those presented by Florenz Ziegfeld:[6] a goal eventually furthered by the advent of color, of which Minnelli was a master), mobilize the spectator's body to an even greater extent than does live theater, given that, although the moviegoer is riveted to his seat, his gaze, in thrall to the images on the screen, is a plaything of the camera's movements, of all manner of editing tricks and ruses.

The effect of being held captive is less apparent when we read a book or listen to a lecture. According to an intellectualist prejudice denounced by Merleau-Ponty, and still current, words and phrases read or heard can have meaning only for active intelligences that try to discern, if not to reconstruct, through them, the thought of the writer or speaker. But isn't it the secret desire of every writer, of every orator, to so captivate the attention of his readers or listeners that they are gripped, almost literally, by his writing or rhetoric, that his text or lecture replaces, if only momentarily, their own thoughts? This would entail a surrender to the text, to the utterance in question. Which presupposes a mode of attention inextricable from a work of memory that is *projective*. Reading or listening to a text requires the same kind of memory that we need to comprehend a single sentence: memory of a kind irreducible to the simple registration of givens or traces that must be interpreted by thought; memory as a function of the future, of the expectation as much as of the promise of a meaning fully grasped only at the end of the period or peroration, but which is already there, present and active, from the first words. In the way that the opening steps of the Central Park dance, however tentative and subdued they might be, however close to walking, anticipate fully the subsequent development that is their confirmation. The transition into the dance sequence[7] is also this: an invitation to the absent body, or, better, to the abstract, suspended, neutralized body of the spectator, a suggestion that he or she surrender to gesticulations whose ultimate meaning has already been clearly established in spoken language. Hunter remarks, with feigned naivete: "Here we are the only animals given the greatest means of communicating, and all we do is snarl at each other." But it is dance, and dance alone, that provides the answer to the question that Gabrielle then puts to him: "Tony, can you and I really dance together?"

Merleau-Ponty, again, regarded speech as true gesture, if not gesticulation, as a mode of communication that comprises its own meaning, just as gesture does.[8] But what about dance? And what about camera movement, which Minnelli saw as related to choreography?[9] The camera, which, instead of remaining stationary in front of the scene it is recording, moves into it, following the dancers' movements, their turns, their *jetés simples* or *battus*, their *glissades*, and almost all their moves (horizontal as well as vertical: in the Central Park dance, Hunter executes effortlessly, if freely, a lift that he had flubbed in rehearsal), all their displacements (which sometimes imply movement from one scene or tableau to another) —in short, far from being intrusive in the way long dreaded by Fred Astaire,[10] it enters actively into the dance. A dance—herein lies all Minnelli's art—in relation to which the camera, without breaking the rhythm or the flow, without impeding the steps executed by the dancers, functions much like a mirror or an echo chamber, mimicking or amplifying each movement. To such an extent that there could be no better example of a "slide into a dance" than the movement of gradual approach that opens the Central Park sequence: from the slow walk through the small open-air dance (but not so as to dance like the couples here, or as they would have danced themselves in one of the nightclubs to which Hunter first offered to take Gabrielle, places where they certainly could have determined whether or not they could be true partners: they needed a site, and a setting, that would likewise participate in the game) to the *glissade* set to the first measures of "Dancing in the Dark," punctuated by a quick turn from Gabrielle, followed immediately, as if in response, by Hunter's turn in the opposite direction, and by another turn from Gabrielle, after which they both remain still for a moment, face to face, feet apart, before beginning their pas de deux, still separated: until the moment when Hunter takes Gabrielle by the hand, sends her into a spin, and leads her, buoyant in her white dress, into a dance that, even after repeated viewings, seems to be taking place *for the first time.*

I should note here how, in the final dance sequence, "The Girl Hunt," the camera, used with relative restraint in the Central Park dance, mimics every turn and swerve, every moment of hesitation or suspense, every avoidance followed by momentary contact or prolonged embrace, every frustrated pursuit, every throw or ground-hugging *glissade*, combining wide-angle shots, forward and backward tracking shots, establishing shots and close-ups. The camera effectively functioning here as another partner, much like the voice-over first-person narration: as if the dance were reduced to an illustration of the story, as if it were the dance that echoed the work—in what person is that?—of the camera. Just as the big numbers listed in the program amount to more or less developed variations on a theme introduced during the scene set in the Central Park hollow, effectively a mold or matrix for the film as a whole. Variations premised on a change of partner or the addition of a third party: when Hunter dances with another woman, the scene begins to resemble a marionette theater or a merry-go-round of automata;[11] when he finds himself with a male partner ("I guess I'll have to change my plans"), they wear the same outfits—tails, top hat, cane—and sing in unison while executing the same steps (even making the same mistakes). When he finds himself reduced to the state of a child along with his two buddies ("Triplets"), wearing bibs and diapers, they all sing, in chorus, how each of them wants a "widduw gun" with which to shoot the others and become the "only one" in front of the camera. But when Hunter dances with his single and unique *partner*, regardless of whether she appears disguised as a blonde or with her "natural" black hair, we are dealing with two different avatars of the same couple: one in which a blonde Gabrielle plays a weak and helpless woman, throwing herself into Hunter's arms; and another in which she plays a "bad" beauty who, already Nicholas

Ray's "party girl," stands up to him—but of the two, the femme fatale turns out not to be the one you'd expected (the same goes for the killer).

The analysis that I have just sketched presupposes, clearly, a relationship with the film different from that based on a single viewing of it. A relationship of familiarity, and one greatly facilitated by video technology. Here again, a matter of *reproduction*, or, as we might also say, of *recording*. For film can now, with regard to dance, effect an operation that would become that of video with regard to film: an operation making it unnecessary for us to rely solely on memories of a performance. In the same way that a recording can make a memorable jazz riff forever accessible (old fan that I am, I still cherish some 78s that are totally worn out in spots because of my having listened over and over to passages that I found especially difficult). But how can we not feel that such reproductions (such recordings) alter the originals so radically as to compromise their character as performances as well as the form of memory operative at the movies, and that confers upon them part of their *aura*?[12]

While Hunter and Gabrielle dance for us on the screen, we have no thoughts: the spectacle of the dance occupies us completely, as when we listen to a solo by Charlie Parker, or a ballad sung by Billie Holiday. Every step, every movement of the two partners holds our attention fully, we sense its necessity despite being unable to predict it. To paraphrase Merleau-Ponty, the end of the dance is the lifting of a spell.[13] Could my "mistake" have resulted from a desire to retain the memory of this spell intact, even if it were distorted, and to keep alive the possibility of its renewal? I must confess that I now know the Central Park dance sequence by heart, as well as "The Girl Hunt" (like certain solos by Parker and Stan Getz), and that this gives me a surplus of pleasure analogous to that produced by a geometric proof: in addition to being struck by the inevitability of each step in succession, as it comes, I now feel a sense of "rightness" about the dance as a whole, and all at once. The theorem in question being that these two were definitely meant to dance together. QED.

That a dance might present itself as a proof or an experiment, even as the expression of a desire (for it is the desire to dance together that drives Hunter and Gabrielle after having too long prevented them from doing so), with the dance itself figuring as demonstration or verification, if not of satisfying a desire: this is but another way of saying that a thought can be at work in a dance much as it can be in dreams. A thought that, however deftly contrived the choreography, is irreducible to a statement, much less to a formula. A thought that can be grasped only through the steps themselves, their description necessarily entailing their inscription or projection, moment by moment, onto the plane of the bodies' trajectories through space. Which explains the intimate relationship between film and dance, one established and secured, from the advent of sound, in musical comedy. The necessity of the ordering of the images, and of the sequence of camera movements and edits, coming to seem increasingly inevitable as the projection proceeds.

The success of movie musicals in their heyday resulted, in the best examples, from a happy rivalry between the progress of the narrative and that of the bodies and images, the dynamic of Minnelli's films, as Deleuze notes, being ultimately more important than their story.[14] A competition that neither precludes nor requires symbiosis, as is clearly demonstrated by "The Girl Hunt" ballet from the moment the curtain rises, or rather—a tribute to a famous shot in Howard Hawks's *The Big Sleep*—from the moment we see the machine gun on the cover of a detective novel, which then vanishes to reveal the set on which the ballet will take place. A ballet recounting, like the musical accompaniment, a private eye's own account of his adventures, a role played by Hunter within the ballet.

"A Murder Mystery in Jazz," reads the subtitle in the program. On the train taking the troupe to New York, Hunter feigns nervousness, asking himself whether he will be up to the challenge. Now it is well known that Fred Astaire was one of those who, from Paul Whiteman to Frank Sinatra by way of George Gershwin, realized very early on how whites could turn black music and related expressive forms to advantage, to the benefit of often dubious "entertainments." The dance number performed by Hunter and a black shoeshine man in a "penny arcade" makes this relationship explicit: it is the black man who shines the white man's shoes ("Shine on Your Shoes"). And Cordova himself, the high-strung director, observes that there's no difference between the "magic rhythms" of Shakespeare's verse and those of "Bill Robinson's immortal feet," celebrated elsewhere by Duke Ellington and the film *Stormy Weather*, to say nothing of Fred Astaire himself.[15] But, beyond the models exploited by Fred Astaire with the aid of his assistant and alter ego, Hermes Pan, short of taps and tap dancing, it is the jazz beat itself, what was then called "swing," that, in rather sweetened form, sometimes plush with violins ("Dancing in the Dark") and sometimes raucous (the brass in "The Girl Hunt"), is the basis for his best numbers, setting his style apart from that of, say, Gene Kelly. The beat of jazz, its swing. But also the beat of the Broadway tunes that often served as a basis for improvisations by jazz musicians, both black and white, as well as for dance numbers. A beat simple and imperious, and that provides the best support for projective memory: from the opening measures of "Dancing in the Dark," the viewer knows that the dance will unfold in accordance with a rigorous, altogether predictable AABA scheme (two verses, a "bridge," and a final verse), with each of the four sections consisting of eight measures, making for a total of thirty-two measures.[16]

In *The Bandwagon*, when Cordova's pretentious production "lays an egg," Hunter decides to rework it, announcing his intention to cut the Faust references and make it jazzier. At which point, as I misremembered (and still remember) the film before seeing it again on video, he says: "Let's jazz it!" But jazz is not the only key element in this transformation: the sets, too, are crucial, as Deleuze notes. In the ballet from *Silk Stockings*, which reworks, to a score by Cole Porter, the plot of *The Bandwagon* ("Fated to Be Mated"), Astaire and Charisse pass through a series of sets, each inferring the kind of dance that indeed unfolds within it: until a moment when, entering what seems to be a rehearsal studio, they come to a stop and, after a moment's hesitation, start walking and then segue into another dance, this one accompanied by a jazz trio (piano, bass, drums), that continues until the end of the piece, the only argument here being the music and the rhythm, swing and the beat, this part of the sequence having been shaped, as we realize instantly, to evoke a jazz ballad. For Rouben Mamoulian here appropriated a strategy used with great subtlety by Minnelli. In the words of Deleuze, which I must quote here at length:

"It fell to Minnelli to discover that dance does not simply give a fluid world to images, but that there are as many worlds as images. . . . The plurality of worlds was Minnelli's first discovery, his very great position in cinema. But how, then, do we pass from one world to another? This is the second discovery; dance is no longer simply movement of world, but passage from one world to another, entry into another world, breaking in and exploring. . . . Each set attains its fullest power, and becomes pure description of world which replaces the situation.[17]

In the matter of description, the sets in *The Bandwagon* help to shape the dynamic of its situations. At the beginning of the film, Hunter leaves Hollywood for Manhattan, the site of his first successes, settling down to work after a short walk down Forty-second Street and through a penny arcade, where, after his shoes have been shined, fortune smiles on him. It is the city, through the intermediary of these sets, that confers on the images what Sartre called their "atmosphere of world." The city that serves as backdrop for the dance in Central Park, that the "private eye" in "The Girl Hunt" explores to its very depths: as far as the subway, where gangsters shoot each other, again in the background. The city, with its skyscrapers and its subway, rendered in black and white in the "Two-Faced Woman" ballet, which corresponds to one of the faces of Gabrielle, whereas Greenwich Village (which has the wan charm of the town in Brigadoon) corresponds to the other. Black and white, brunette and blonde: this number, which, thanks to my mistake, I saw only once during the broadcast, would have been decidedly out of place in *The Bandwagon*. For, in the end, Hunter opts for the urban, worldly type, for the image of the black-haired Cyd Charisse and of the world—or should we say the scene?—that it entails. A world, a scene that is essentially urban. For only in the city can a setting or scene be an entire world, even if one devised for "entertainment." In a city (especially New York), or at the movies (especially American ones).

The Unconscious in Its Gardens

In his *Introductory Lectures on Psycho-Analysis*, Freud, when he broaches the role of what he calls *Fantasie* (fantasy) in the psychic economy, risks a comparison that has both topographical and institutional resonances:

Thus in the activity of phantasy human beings continue to enjoy the freedom from external compulsion which they have long since renounced in reality. They have contrived to alternate between remaining an animal of pleasure and being once more a creature of reason. Indeed, they cannot subsist on the scanty satisfaction which they can extort from reality. . . . The creation of the mental realm of phantasy finds a perfect parallel in the establishment of "reservations" or "nature reserves" in places where the requirements of agriculture, communications and industry threaten to bring about changes in the original face of the earth which will quickly make it unrecognizable. A nature reserve preserves its original state which everywhere else has to our regret been sacrificed to necessity. Everything, including what is useless and even what is noxious, can grow and proliferate there as it pleases. The mental realm of phantasy is just such a reservation withdrawn from the reality principle.[1]

The comparison is topographical to the extent that it imparts a spatial dimension to the division between the two great principles governing mental life, the pleasure principle and the reality principle. But its institutional resonance, however implicit, also calls for comment. Far from being subject to the reality principle, the creation of "reserves," even if these are declared "natural," presupposes work, part political and part legislative, and often a fierce struggle, as well as investments and sacrifices, more or less large, on both the individual and collective levels. As is all too well known, "freedom" (if such is the appropriate word here) has its price, which is sometimes high. But above all it must be conquered, *instituted*, which entails coming to terms with the law, becoming accustomed to constraint and even, eventually, forming an alliance with it—as happened, in the United States, with the establishment in 1908 of the National Conservation Commission, followed in 1916 by that of the National Parks Service, an agency designed specifically to oversee these "reserves."

America as the scene of its own future life as well as of that of others, but also the scene, for itself if not for others, of a previous life, of a life outside of history, and one heedless of the way consciousness organizes its relations to the past, the present, and the future. Freud apparently became aware of the campaign to establish a system of national parks while visiting the United States in 1909—during which trip he scarcely had time for tourism, apart from a visit to Niagara Falls and a four-day stay at the farm of the neurologist James Johnson Putnam near Lake Placid, which is now in the Adirondacks National Park. He never abandoned his prejudice against America and Americans ("America is a mistake," he told Ernest Jones, "a tremendous mistake, it is true, but a mistake nonetheless"), but this only makes his interest in the project all the more remarkable. In 1911, he alluded to the existence of such parks in a note to "Formulations on the Two Principles in Mental Functioning," mentioning what is still the most famous of them. And this in order to illustrate the process whereby, after the introduction of the reality principle, a split develops in the mental apparatus, manifesting itself in the elaboration of a fantasy life independent of reality testing and regulated exclusively by the pleasure principle, just as "a nation whose wealth rests on the exploitation of the produce of its soil will yet set aside certain areas for reservation in their original state [*im Urstande*] and for protection from the changes brought about by civilization (e.g. Yellowstone Park)."[2]

The necessary complicity of the legislative power in this process was not a matter of concern for Freud, who noted in the same article of 1911 that "substitution of the reality principle for the pleasure principle implies no deposing [*keine Absetzung*] of the pleasure principle, but only a safeguarding of it [*sondern nur eine Sicherung desselben*]"[3]—if only by inflecting or "sublimating" it. Surely the American example interested him, first of all, because it was without precedent or equivalent. But also because its context and premises differed radically from those that presided over the creation, less recent and less symbolically charged, of "natural" parks on the other side of the Atlantic. Old Europe had long since boasted gardens that were open to the public (more or less), and even parks whose designers contrived to compete with nature, but these were conceived in terms of subduing it, of making it conform to the regular patterns associated with French gardens, or of creating "picturesque" prospects that rivaled natural views, featuring, along secluded paths and set into thickets, occasional pavilions, monuments, and artificial ruins. Much the same could be said—despite the differences between European and Far Eastern traditions—of Japanese gardens, which were generally conceived, in terms of both appearance and purpose, as "natural landscapes," with an emphasis on the first word. Japanese gardens are contrived primarily to "be seen," not as scenes or theaters for various activities; the artfulness of their design is meant to be as inconspicuous as possible, everything being arranged such that spectators contemplating them from galleries or verandas, and individuals slowly walking through them, are presented with landscape images that, while composed of specific means and materials, are nonetheless intended to function as fragments of a whole: of nature, of the world, of the universe.[4] Such is not the case, at least in principle, with American national parks.

At least in principle. For their purpose remains, even today, far from clear. As with Manhattanism as reconstituted by Rem Kool-haas,[5] a good part of the "preservationist" ideology long remained unconscious; and the periodic disputes over the national parks only underscore the contradictions implicit in their institution from their inception, contradictions that could not help but leave their mark on the very sites that the new agency had been charged with preserving, for it was also charged with making them suitable for public leisure and recreation, which necessarily entails certain adjustments.[6] The argument advanced in Congress prior to its vote, in the middle of the Civil War, to donate to the state of California, "for the use, so-journ, and recreation of the public," a portion of what would eventually become Yosemite National Park, this argument is surprising, insofar as it invokes one of the most revered sites of the "picturesque" ideology: according to the project's advocates, Yosemite Valley was more *scenic* (and more theatrical) than the Swiss Alps. A setting whose most striking feature was its skyline, "the profile of its horizon"—in a word, what Benjamin would call its *aura*.[7] At least the counterargument advanced by many congressmen had the merit of concision: "not one cent for scenery." But it failed to take into account the gains that would accrue from such an action, if only in terms of representation, as in the use of Monument Valley as a setting for Hollywood westerns. Through such images as the grand compositions of the painter Albert Bierstadt, one of the first to visit Yosemite, and the topographical photographs of Timothy O'Sullivan (documentary in intention), America would discover that it, too, had its monuments: geological ones.[8]

Legend has it that the officer leading a party of cavalrymen in punitive expedition against a band of Yosemite Indians could not, upon entering the valley that now bears the tribe's name, contain his enthusiasm, and immediately expressed a wish that the place be protected from the avarice of some and the vandalism of others. Likewise, the first idea for Yellowstone Park is said to date back to a night in 1870, when a group of explorers, gathered around a campfire, decided that such a treasure must not be allowed to fall into private hands. Which instantly raises the question as to why, at the very moment of discovery, the idea and the wish for "preservation" should have arisen. We owe to Frederick Law Olmstead, one of the designers of New York's Central Park, a surprisingly early report on the conservation and exploitation of the Yosemite Valley, intended for the eyes of Congress (which never saw it): according to him, the place should be preserved for its scenery and its capacity to stimulate intense personal response, the latter often unconscious, a project that would entail safeguarding its natural appearance and minimizing all "artificial construction," inescapably coercive, obliging all visitors to adhere to itineraries devised for them by others, for such interventions would be at odds with the essence of the site: an untamed wildness conducive to contemplation.[9] Conversely, the project establishing Yellowstone Park was passed by Congress in 1872 not because of a few beautiful souls but at the instigation of none other than the Northern Pacific Railroad Company, the site being set aside "as a public or pleasuring ground for the benefit and enjoyment of the people," and the railroad company being designated its principal concessioner, authorized to provide tourists with access as well as with all appropriate services.[10]

Thus "scenery," ideological as much as technological, was in question from the beginning, if unconsciously. The same institution that was intended to make it possible for individuals whose autonomy was threatened by accelerated development and unbridled industrialization to escape, for a time (that of brief vacations devoted to what can already be called "tourism"), from social constraints, this same institution was endorsed, from the start, by the very railroad companies that were, with mass tourism, the first and principal agents of what Alan Trachtenberg has called, in a very great book, "the incorporation of America." "Incorporation" being understood here in both its geographic and its big-business sense: the merger into a single corpus or body, at federal urging, of states hitherto divided, and the progressive expansion of this body across a continent that still seemed like a coat too big for it; the said merger being accompanied by the transition, begun prior to the Civil War, from an agrarian society to an essentially industrial and commercial one modeled, even on the smallest scale, after the corporate system, the emerging network of large, anonymous, highly competitive corporations—its monopolistic tendencies were already apparent—whose establishment was inextricably linked to westward expansion.[11]

According to the myth of the "frontier," given its classic formulation by the historian Frederick Jackson Turner in 1893 (thereby effectively signing its death certificate), the West represented for the young Republic a seemingly inexhaustible reserve of space, if not of territory, where individual initiative could be given free course so long as its boundary continued to be pushed westward (again bringing to mind Hadrian's Wall, which marked the extreme limit of the Roman world, not to mention the Berlin Wall, whose construction signaled the end of Soviet expansionism[12]). A space, a territory regarded as "virgin," its first occupants having no status under the law because they lacked legitimate proof of property ownership, the federal government having taken nominal possession of it before turning it over to private hands as settlement proceeded. The Homestead Act of 1862 stipulated the allocation of 160 acres of public land, in exchange for ten dollars, to any American citizen who applied for it. However, historical research has largely discredited the liberal catch-phrase and myth of the self-made man: in fact, scarcely 10 percent of the land thereby made available to the public was purchased by homesteaders, the balance having been appropriated by the states and by large corporations, beginning with the railroad companies, which could then sell it off at high prices to entrepreneurs wealthier than would-be farmers and ranchers.[13] So the natural resources of the West, minable ones as well as natural (wood from the great forests of California was of unequaled quality), animal, and agricultural resources (large herds of buffalo whose massacre deprived the Indians of a principal means of subsistence, until the legend of western cattle ranchers came to an end in the slaughterhouses of Chicago, and that of the pioneers in the grain silos of the Great Lakes region) were, from the start, designated for exploitation on an industrial scale.

Alan Trachtenberg has exposed the implacable logic of a process that found its first illustration in the irresistible expansion of the network of railroads over paths tread shortly before by animals, which was accompanied by the stringing of telegraph lines along their length, the routes over which information flowed limning those taken by men and merchandise. Until the day when the implacable westward advance of "civilization" was short-circuited by the California gold rush, which occasioned rejection of continental routes in favor of more rapid passage directly to the West Coast: in America, the East, once the Great Lakes had been passed, effectively became the West, the direction of conquest having been effectively reversed at a certain point, a development that rang down the curtain on the myth of the frontier. From that day forward, the "wild" space that originally confronted Americans, and in relation to which they never ceased to define themselves, was no longer situated along the infinitely expandable edge of "civilized" space but rather in its gaps, in its lacunae. Which is to say on sites —encompassed by an ever tightening communications network, such as the "bubbles" of wildness that the said civilization resolved to preserve in its bosom, cognate terms being used to designate both natural "reserves" and the "reservations" within which were henceforth confined the survivors of the various Indian tribes and nations—which the Dawes Act of 1887 presented with the "choice" of either renouncing their wild state in favor of American citizenship (in which case they could, under the Homestead Act, purchase land on which they agreed to live) or trying to preserve something of their traditions and their culture. But, here again, the tourist industry and the ego-ideal that are so crucial to American culture had to be taken into account. For although this project was implemented only after indigenous cultures had been all but wiped out, it had been formulated half a century before, as early as the first displacements of Indian tribes east of the Mississippi, when George Catlin—the explorer and painter whose works, now avidly sought-after by American museums, evidence his interest in native populations that were then disappearing—proposed that vast forests such as he had admired along the banks of the Missouri should be set aside, by appropriate legislation, for preservation in all their wildness and natural beauty, so as to constitute "a *nation's park*" in which the entire world could contemplate, for centuries to come, Indians wearing their traditional dress, galloping on their wild horses through herds of elk and buffalo.[15]

From reservation to preservation, then, and to what is most specific to the most "refined" culture, as well as to the relation the latter means to sustain with nature, even with "wildness."[16] We have seen how Freud hoped to clarify the nature of the life of the "soul" or "psyche" by resorting to images that are essentially visual, by making urban "scenery" contend with that of natural parks and vice versa. To be sure, cities, in their "historical" aspect, have need of preservationist measures analogous to those implemented in "natural" parks, since they function, in many respects, on the level of myth as well as on that of tourism and Saturday night fever: as "pleasure reserves," when they are not theaters of violence that is soon repressed. Even so, images of the city and of natural parks seem to be situated, to use a spatial metaphor, at opposite poles. The mountaintops and cliffs in Yosemite Park can function, in visual terms, as another kind of skyline, whereas the arbors of Central Park are so many hollows, resembling a giant gap in the grid of Manhattan, against the New York skyline. Cities, in the course of their uncontrolled development, can begin to resemble something natural, whereas so-called natural parks are themselves far from being "without" or "outside of history," being as traversed by it as they are by their many paths and roads. Yet both present images of an inverted relation between time and space: archaeology tries to translate into temporal terms the strata that have accumulated over centuries on sites that are or were occupied by a city; the institution of a "natural" park or reserve is intended to restore time to space and to inscribe within geography reference to a temporality prior or foreign to that of history—at least as this term is generally understood in the West, and especially in America, which strives to reconstitute within its bosom reserves of the wildness and the space that it initially represented for Europe, before coming to function, as a discursive event, as Europe's unconscious. To such an extent that the discourse on the city and the discourse on national parks are like entries in an inventory of one and the same place. A place of thought, a place of power; a place of thought in its relation to power; a place of power in its relation to thought; a place attesting to the thought of power; a place attesting to the power or powers of thought. The power that thought can have over things, and first of all over places, the city and its supposed antithesis, the natural reserve. But the power, as well, that it (thought) can extract from all those sites through which passes what is now known as "history," which encompass the latter's relation to the unconscious.

"[The] psyche is extended," Freud noted, but "knows nothing of this." Extension is a characteristic feature of the psyche, even its very substance, but only insofar as it remains unaware of this, only insofar as this feature, this substance, remains oblivious of its being a feature, if not the very substance, of the unconscious. The psyche; but history? If Freud's discovery of the unconscious took place in a context marked by the then predominant theory of cerebral localizations, and if the first topography of the psychic apparatus—as described by Freud in his *Entwurf einer Psychologie* (Project for a Scientific Psychology) of 1895 and in letters written to Fliess in 1896 —was still based on the neurological apparatus,[17] the tone for this had already been established, in the United States, in literature associated with the development of railroad and telegraph networks (not to mention the network of telephone lines that would soon follow), and more generally with the westward march that Frederick Jackson Turner himself compared to the regular growth of a complex nervous system gradually extending itself across a continent that previously had been "simple" and "inert." Mechanical metaphors spread rapidly among doctors, from Oliver Wendell Holmes, who was so bold as to proclaim in 1870 that "the more we examine the mechanism of thought, the more we shall see that the automatic, unconscious action of the mind enters largely into all its processes," to George Beard and his work on the neurasthenia and other nervous disturbances induced by modern life and, more precisely, by the communications industry: like the electric generator devised by Edison (a friend of Beard's), the nervous system resembled the center from which energy fueling all of the organs was dispensed, "modern nervousness" being a translation of the "complaints" of a system exposed to the assaults of the telegraph, the railroad, and the printing press.[18]

"Nervousness" as a mark of distinction: as Alan Trachtenberg notes, the neurasthenia described by Beard as "American" affected only the elite that was struggling for wealth and power. But an elite that, also, was in possession of the intellectual and financial means, and the leisure time, effectively required of those visiting the first national parks. As long as tourism remained an option limited to a small number of people willing to accept relatively primitive lodgings and interested primarily in contemplation, the symbolic stakes at issue in the creation and preservation of "natural reserves" did not seem threatened. Things changed radically with the advent of mass tourism, thanks to which, with help from the automobile (and the attendant parking lots and traffic jams), elements of urban life were introduced into the parks: shops, nightlife, and rows of trailers and recreational vehicles in which tourists could recover from their daytime exertions while watching television—all arrayed against a superb scenic backdrop. The debate over what has mockingly been called "Yosemite City" is far from over: in Greece, very few have spoken out against the transformation of Cape Sounion into a Las Vegas for the poor—replete with nightclubs made of cinder blocks and undulating sheet metal—that effectively reduces the ruins of the temple of Poseidon and the view of the Mediterranean to mere backdrop, to something resembling, by a curious reversal, and thanks to neon lighting, a decoration at Caesars Palace.

At the beginning of this chapter, I noted the topographical and institutional resonances of the "natural reserve" metaphor. However contradictory these two aspects might seem, they nonetheless correspond to a transition or passage—one among many that are possible—between the preeminently descriptive approach I have used in the preceding exercises and what would be a *topique* or "topos" in the narrow sense: a *theory*, as I said at the outset, and not merely an inventory of places. A theory beginning, in this case, at the point where the analogy functions in reverse, against the grain, and where the Freudian topography, far from merely using visual images, begins to strive to clarify the way they function, and to render more precise what is at stake in them, which is essentially symbolic. And to do this without holding to a fixed notion of psychic place, but by attending as closely as possible to the conceptual shifts that prepared the transition from the first Freudian topography to the second, with its division of the unconscious into the id, the ego, and the superego. Insofar as, chronologically as well as theoretically speaking, Freud's reference to American national parks is inscribed very precisely in this context, which, in turn, confers all of its weight upon his analogy.

Sticking with the notion of the "ego-ideal," which, as is well known, played an important role in the elaboration of the notion of the superego and, more generally, of the second theory of the psychic apparatus, the juxtaposition of the narcissistic element and the collective element, and the imbrication of the two aspects—ideal and prohibition—described by Freud in *The Ego and the Id*,[19] effectively recurs in the debate over national parks: as understood early on by Olmstead and John Muir, the other apostle of Yosemite Park, when Americans leave their vehicles to explore the redwood forests of Mariposa Grove or to raft down the Colorado, they reconnect, on the level of fantasy, with the exploits and activities of the pioneers, whereas in nonnational, commercial "parks" such as Disneyland visitors are completely subservient to the machinery of the place. Even so, the idea of an inviolate nature, one whose wildness is untamed, is less simple that Freud would have us believe: aside from the fact that it was integral to the first Americans' image of their own reality, it is premised less on the pleasure principle than on values that are not necessarily shared by the population as a whole, but that advocates of the "preservationist" ideology hold to be corollaries of the "American dream" (a phrase whose linkage of fantasy with the ideal makes it especially apt in this context). And this not without the imposition of very strict rules on visitors, primarily for ethical and symbolic reasons, lending credence to the notion, advanced by Freud, of a possible reconciliation between the two principles, under the double aegis of education (which he described as an incitement to prevail over the pleasure principle so as to abet, through all manner of incentives, ego development) and of art, which gives form to fantasy by converting it into reality of another order:[20] a reality—as evidenced by the first images produced by painters and photographers of the sites being considered for preservation—that is essentially "scenic," and that Americans had to appropriate so as to produce *their* scene, the "American scene," America as "scene," a project well worth the expenditure of a few "cents."

Thus, as Freud suggested, the creation of a psychic realm of "fantasy" and the institution of national parks are perfectly analogous: both satisfy the same need, topographical if ever one was, to see constituted, as a reaction against the exigencies of the reality principle as manifested in mental life as well as in geography, a domain and a field of activities free of its grip. With the caveat that the "animal of pleasure" to which the parks were meant to appeal is supposed to cohabit peaceably with the "rational animal," and that the pleasures "reserved" for them both are directly related to what might be called the "American" ego-ideal, if these are not its immediate issue. At the time Freud was writing, America was perhaps no longer the agrarian society that was described to him. Nonetheless, he heard the message addressed to him and managed to translate it into his own terms. "Natural reserves" were intended to perpetuate a primitive state that could survive only in the guise of isolated islands inscribed on maps like so many holes or pieces inlaid after the fact, as in a clumsy patchwork, and suggestive of a body in pieces. Everything about the history of America's national parks confirms this: their first defenders were not ecologists *avant la lettre* but moralists and promoters, if not savvy businessmen; and, contrary to myth, their setting aside of these tracts did not so much precede or anticipate advances in agriculture, communications, and industry as issue from their very excesses, from their brutality, from their precipitous tempo. At issue was nothing less than America's image of itself, if not the very meaning of the word "America." "A word," to cite Alan Trachtenberg, "whose meaning became the focus of controversy and struggle during an age in which the horrors of civil war remained vivid. In the eyes of those farmers, laborers, and radicals who joined in the People's Party of the 1890s, America incorporated represented a misappropriation of the name."[21] The appearance of discontinuity, even dismemberment, created by inscribing park boundaries on maps and assigning these tracts different colors is a consequence of the brutal juxtaposition of the two bodies, no longer of the king,[22] but of the young American republic: its institutional body, its constituted body, in the sense that a state or a corporation is constituted; and its mythical body, ostensibly primitive or "wild," of which the national parks are so many relics, still active, still efficacious.

Of these two bodies, could it be said that one is dedicated to time and the other to space, despite its being answerable to a "prehistory" not without its relevance to the history of America? Frederick Jackson Turner saw in the "frontier" the surest means of assimilating the composite population that would become the American people. In this process, the earth itself had a role a play, figuring in it as an independent character. "The wilderness masters the colonist," he wrote, evoking a ritual central to American literature from Fenimore Cooper to Faulkner and Hemingway: the pioneer's literal "descent," after having discarded his European clothing, from the railroad platform to the canoe, his entry into the wild (in the sense of entering a dance the mobilizes one's entire body), and the ascesis whereby he eventually transforms the land, progressively remaking it in his own image—"the meeting point between savagery and civilization" becoming an indispensable reference point for *homo americanus*.[23] The "frontier" having ceased to fulfill its role, the birth of the American nation presupposed the setting aside of parks not so much "natural" as *national* to serve as a "backdrop" against which could rise the figure of America and, with it, figures that would inscribe themselves "in reserve" in the body of the nation, the national parks being, in their way, an instrument of its symbolic "incorporation." The essential thing, from the point of view adopted here, being this exchange or mixture, this permanent conversion of time into space and of space into time: the railroad, by inexorably spreading its network over the spaces of the West, would oblige America, through the need for reliable timetables, to adopt a *standard time* that would henceforth govern all human activity;[24] while creation of the national parks satisfied the old American dream of a history that has accrued a geological dimension and a sedimented time, inscribed from the start in space, a time *that has taken place.*

In these reserves, Freud writes, "Everything, including what is useless and even what is noxious, can grow and proliferate . . . as it pleases. The mental realm of phantasy is just such a reservation withdrawn from the reality principle." The unconscious has its gardens, which are usually left fallow. But the realm of fantasy nonetheless functions in them as a scene for willfully labyrinthine games calculated in accordance with an algebra that is sometimes mad, even delirious, but that nonetheless has its laws; whereas the unconscious, however "without history" (but not without laws) it is said to be, presents itself as the most originary site of this same articulation between human becoming and so-called natural history, which is illustrated by the development of great urban agglomerations. Without taking into account the fact that phantasmatic activity need not deck itself out in luxuriant forms, that it can accommodate itself to a nature that is severe and stingy, so long as the latter is not miserly with space, the wilderness logically taking the place of the national parks in the social imaginary, in their capacity as "natural" reserves. With the caveat that, here again, the desertlike spaces of the American West seem to inscribe themselves within a temporality that is radically other: the giant sequoias of northern California seem so gigantic as to have first "sprouted from the seed" at a moment contemporary with the Trojan War, in myth effectively the inaugural episode of European history;[25] while there is nothing ancient or sublime about the brush and cacti of the desert—nothing, at least, that might warrant their inscription within "history," of whatever duration.

America is the only "Western" country to encompass within its territory vast regions that appear on maps as splotches designating so many deserts. The only country, too, in the entire world, to become concerned early on about the fate of these deserts, even if for reasons that, again, were not always clear, or that would only be too much so (remember Chateaubriand: "Her wilderness will be her manners"). For the desert can be the site of experiences very different from those —personal as well as professional—related by Reyner Banham in a book conceived in the great British tradition of accounts of travels through the deserts of the ancient world: *Scenes in America Deserta*, which narrates the various ways in which the author, an architectural historian by profession, learned as much there about himself (and about his unconscious) as about the natural phenomena of the sites that he describes. Sites that, true to expectation, sometimes lent themselves to architectural exercises: whether Frank Lloyd Wright's Taliesin West complex, long used as a place of work and indoctrination by Wright, he who dreamed of seeing his low-density development scheme, Broadacre City, spread across the entire continent, transforming America into a kind of endless suburb within whose interstices would be national parks, including the *abstract* lands, spaces, sites that, in his view, were its deserts; or, conversely, but in the same geographical vicinity, the hyperconcentrated utopian habitat conceived by his disciple Paolo Soleri, which would logically have found its place, as Banham notes, like experimental detonations of the atom bomb, in places where no one would see them or exercise the least censorship over them:[26] in one of these deserts, precisely, which in the view of this agnostic Englishman had the additional advantage of having nothing to do with the Bible (whereas references to the Promised Land are rarely absent from texts about the American West and the national parks[27]).

The activity of the National Wilderness Preservation System nonetheless raises a question for thought from the moment that, in its very governing principle, it seems to run counter to Nietzsche's admonition: "The wilderness grows. Woe unto him that harbors wildernesses!"[28] Was Heidegger not right to stress the connection between this passage and that aspect of our time which has given us most pause, not because of the dehumanization of the world (which would be a contradiction in terms, there being no world save in reference to humanity) but because of its accelerated devastation, and the seemingly implacable desolation that accompanies it? Its being admitted—as we read in *What Is Called Thinking?*, the entire first part of which turns on Nietzsche's three words: "The wilderness grows"—that "the African Sahara is only one kind of wasteland" among many, and that "the devastation of the earth can easily go hand in hand with a guaranteed supreme living standard for man, and just as easily with the organized establishment of a uniform state of happiness for all men: not all deserts result from accumulations of sand."[29] Proof that the protection of natural deserts might seem to assert itself as an antidote against a general desolation henceforth spreading into virgin areas, in the guise, among many others, of vehicular rodeos that bring together in the Mojave Desert, some distance from Las Vegas, thousands of motorcycles and SUVs. Not to mention experiences otherwise disquieting for humanity, for all that, as noted by Hannah Arendt, the word "experiment" still has any meaning after having been used to designate nuclear tests, whose effects are so large-scale that, no matter how remote the site on which they are carried out, "their laboratory coincides with the globe."[30]

"The wilderness grows. Woe unto him who harbors wildernesses!" This remark, which Nietzsche placed in the mouth of a traveler who calls himself Zarathustra's shadow, is, however, fraught with ambiguity. Heidegger warns us: "But riddle upon riddle: what was once the scream 'The Wasteland grows . . .' now threatens to turn into chatter."[31] Chatter, a way of speaking—of describing what is "by its nature . . . indescribable, because it lends itself to being thought about only in a thinking that is a kind of appeal, a call—and therefore must at times become a scream"[32]—adopted by Hannah Arendt herself when she described California and its universities as "a sublime desert, the most sublime of all deserts," and when she taught a course at Berkeley entitled "From Desert to Oasis,"[33] even as she observed, as I have above, that at this extreme point of our Western world, "the Orient (China) is no longer in the east but in the west."[34] Still a kind of blink fraught with consequences for thinking, and which sets limits for it. For the desert has its oases: oases where the same sky—as Nietzsche's "wanderer" sings —that is moist and melancholy for old Europe, as it often is in northern California, the first Orient, is clear and cloudless. But Nietzsche's curse (that of the "shadow of Zarathustra") was aimed less at lovers of oases (and of the young girls that they shelter, children "profound but without thoughts," comparable to those scripted enigmas, fortune cookies, served after dinner in Chinese restaurants in America) than at those seeking to preserve the desert itself, even to carry it into their innermost selves. For while there can be no oases without the desert, the reverse does not hold. The "moral lion" might well roar at girls of the desert, but the singer knew what was important: "For virtuous howling . . . is more than anything else European fervor, European ravenous hunger!"[35] If the curse was directed first, as Heidegger maintained, if not against Nietzsche himself, then at least against those to whom it would fall to break with Old Man, the man of tradition, that is because the superman for whose advent Zarathustra prayed would of necessity be fascinated by the desert, much as philosophers remain, despite themselves, fascinated by the labyrinth. The desert—including the threat that it harbors, and the resistance born of the desire and mortal horror that it inspires—being all too conducive to *thinking*.

Deserts—beginning with those of the "new world"—would thus be, for better and worse, last places where anything able to grow or happen there does so free of all constraints save natural ones: anything, including that which is useless or noxious, beginning with the most dubious and destructive products of industrial society. Last places in the sense that Nietzsche spoke of the "last man," he whom the superman would surpass, would exceed, would *repress*, but whom he harbors within himself, just as he harbors his own passing away (hence the wanderer's curse).[36] The territory, the scene par excellence of fantasy, but strictly programmed, this fantasy, even though the spectacles offered by the desert cannot always be located on maps, nor do they always satisfy the pleasure animal within man (Rimbaud, that too hurried and unhappy prototype of the Nietzschean superman, proved this in spades, in Harrar and elsewhere[37]). But, also, the most fascinating and formidable of labyrinths, at least in Herodotus's sense of the word. As was known to the king of the Arabs whose story Borges recounts to us, and who, by way of revenge against the king of Babylonia—who had maliciously left him to his own devices in a bronze labyrinth with countless stairways, walls, and doors—once having captured him, showed him his own labyrinth, which had neither stairways to climb, nor doors to force, nor walls to impede his passage: "Then he untied the bonds of the king and abandoned him in the middle of the desert, where he died of hunger and thirst."[38] After what wanderings, after what detours, at the limit of what despair the story does not say.

Notes

PREFACE

1. Sigmund Freud, *Gesammelte Werke* (hereafter *GW*), 17:132; *Standard Edition* (hereafter *SE*) 23 (1964):300 [translation modified].

2. Friedrich Nietzsche, *Thus Spake Zarathustra*, Part II ("On Redemption"), *The Portable Nietzsche*, ed. and trans. Walter Kaufmann (New York: Viking Press, 1954), 251.

3. J[ohan] Gunnar Andersson, *Children of the Yellow Earth: Studies in Prehistoric China*, trans. E. Classen (Cambridge, Mass.: MIT Press [1973]), xvii–xviii, 94–95 [translation modified]. First published London, 1934.

4. Paul Valéry, *Oeuvres*, 2 vols. (Paris: Bibliothèque de la Pléiade, 1960), 2:804.

5. Paul Valéry, *Eupalinos; or, The Architect*, trans. William M. Stewart (London: Oxford University Press, 1932), 21.

6. Ibid., 9.

7. Paul Valéry, "Mexican" notebook (1900–1901), in *Cahiers 1894–1914* (Paris: Gallimard, 1992), 4:74.

8. Valéry, "Les deux vertus d'un livre," *Pièces sur l'art*, in *Oeuvres*, 2:1247.

CHAPTER I

1. Descartes, *Discourse on the Method*, in *The Philosophical Writings of Descartes*, trans. John Cottingham, Robert Stoothoff, and Dugald Murdoch, 2 vols. (Cambridge: Cambridge University Press, 1985), 1:116.

2. Descartes, *Méditations métaphysiques*, in *Oeuvres* (Paris: Bibliothèque de la Pléiade, 1952), 281. Compare Descartes, *Meditations on First Philosophy*, in ibid., 2:21. [Damisch uses the French text, whereas the cited English translation by John Cottingham (currently the most authoritative one) is based on the original Latin version.—Trans.]

3. Descartes, *Discours de la méthode*, in *Oeuvres*, 145. Compare Des-

cartes, *Discourse on the Method,* in *The Philosophical Writings of Descartes,* 1:125.

4. Colin Rowe and Fred Koetter, *Collage City* (Cambridge, Mass.: MIT Press, 1978), 42–46.

5. Descartes, *Discourse on the Method,* 117.

6. Anthony Vidler, *Claude-Nicolas Ledoux: Architecture and Social Reform at the End of the Ancien Régime* (Cambridge, Mass., and London: MIT Press, 1990).

7. Adrien Baillet, *Vie de M. Descartes* (Paris: Plon, 1946), 79–80. First published 1691.

8. I have shown elsewhere that the first "perspective views" were views of cities, sometimes—rightly—said to be "ideal," not in a utopian sense but in a mathematical one, insofar as they invite various operations pertinent to the process of idealization. See Hubert Damisch, *The Origin of Perspective,* trans. John Goodman (Cambridge, Mass.: MIT Press, 1994).

9. In William Dean Howells's novel *A Hazard of New Fortunes* (1890), the protagonist, looking at New York City from a car of the "elevated," is suddenly overtaken by a feeling that the world is both godless and lawless, a place whose disorder speaks of an absence of planning and intelligence.

10. *"Ein ökonomisches Kunstwerk"*: Karl Marx, *Capital,* Book I, Chapter 5.

11. Walter Benjamin, "A Small History of Photography," in *One Way Street and Other Writings,* trans. Edmund Jephcott and Kingsley Shorter (London: New Left Books, 1979), 256 [translation modified].

12. Edgar Allan Poe, "The Man of the Crowd," *The Complete Works of Edgar Allan Poe,* ed. James A. Harrison, 17 vols. (New York: AMS Press, Inc., 1965), 4:136. Compare French translation by Charles Baudelaire (*Oeuvres en prose* [Paris: Bibliothèque de la Pléiade, 1951], 312): "comme s'ils se sentaient seuls par le fait même de la multitude qui les entourait"; cited by Walter Benjamin in *The Arcades Project,* trans. Howard Eiland and Kevin McLaughlin (Cambridge, Mass., and London: The Belknap Press of Harvard University Press, 1999), 445 (convolute M15a, 2).

13. "The masses in Baudelaire. They stretch before the flâneur as a veil: they are the newest drug for the solitary.—Second, they efface all traces of the individual: they are the newest asylum for the reprobate and the proscript" (Benjamin, *The Arcades Project,* 446 [convolute M16, 3]).

14. Ibid. (convolute M16, 3).

15. See Marcel Roncayolo, *La Ville et ses territoires* (Paris: Gallimard, 1990), 21.

16. On this point, see below, Chap. 6.

17. See Gerald Edelman, *Biologie de la conscience* (Paris: Odile Jacob, 1992).

18. Freud, *Civilization and Its Discontents*, in *SE*, 21 (1961):70–71.

19. See Rowe and Koetter (as in note 4, above).

20. See Roncayolo (as in note 15, above); Bernard Lepetit and Denise Pumain, eds., *Temporalités urbaines* (Paris: Economica, 1993).

CHAPTER 2

1. Herodotus, *The History*, trans. David Grene (Chicago and London: University of Chicago Press, 1987), 145 (2.35).

2. See Camille Sourdille, *La Durée et l'Étendue du voyage d'Hérodote en Égypte* (Paris: n.p., 1910), 147–49.

3. Herodotus, 196 (2.148)

4. Ibid., 145 (2.35).

5. Ibid., 196 (2.148).

6. Ibid., 195 (2.147).

7. Strabo, *Geography*, trans. H. L. Jones, 8 vols. (Cambridge, Mass.: Harvard University Press, Loeb Classical Library, 1917–32), 8 (1932):103–5 (17.1.37).

8. French-language edition of Herodotus's *History* ed. and trans. Ph. Legrand (Paris: Les Belles Lettres, 1972), 169, n. 5. The labyrinth could be the work, even the immense funerary temple, of Amenemhet III (also known as Moeris), whose name has been discovered in the ruins and of whom the immense adjacent pyramid (Hawara, opened by F. Petrie) was the tomb (see Sourdille, as in note 2, above).

9. Pliny the elder, *Natural History*, trans. H. Rackham, W. H. S. James, and D. F. Eichholz , 10 vols. (Cambridge, Mass.: Harvard University Press, Loeb Classical Library, 1938–1962), 10 (1962):66–73 (Book XXXVI, 84–91).

10. Ibid., 69 (XXXVI, 86). The marble in question is the very white limestone of Egypt, which Theophrastus compared to Parian marble (*de Lap.* 7). In the New Kingdom, the complex, which was still intact when Strabo saw it, housed lime kilns. *Syenite* stone in fact designates granite from Aswan (see commentary by A. Rouveret in the French translation of Pliny, *Histoire naturelle*, trans. R. Bloch (Paris: Les Belles Lettres, 1981), 192).

11. Ibid., 68–71 (XXXVI, 87–89). As indicated by A. Rouveret in the French edition (see note 10, above), Pliny misunderstood the word *pteron*, which designates not a special elevated construction outside the labyrinth but large walls enclosing the pronaos, or temple forecourt.

12. Ibid., 70–73 (XXXVI, 90).

13. See below, Chap. 5.

14. Alois Riegl has deftly evoked the way Egyptian architecture, despite the amplitude of its interior volumes, tends to destroy all feeling of open, unencumbered space through the multiplication of columns that he thought to be without structural function, whereas temples are subdivided into a multiplicity of microcosms that are themselves full of columns. *Late Roman Art Industry*, trans. Rolf Winkes (Rome: G. Bretschneider, 1985), 27–28. First published in German in 1927.

15. On this point, and on the Cretan labyrinth generally and the fact that the myth plays systematically on relations between figure and ground, since Daedalus could only have been the architect if he was also the inventor of statuary, see Hubert Damisch, "La danse de Thésée" in *Ruptures/ Cultures* (Paris: Éditions de Minuit, 1976), 163–75.

16. On modern interpretations of the Hawara complex, see A. Rouveret in the French edition of Pliny cited above in n. 10, 190–91, n. 4. All of the classical texts dealing with the Egyptian labyrinth are lucidly discussed in Paolo Santarcangeli, *Il Libro dei labirinti* (Milan: n.p., 1984), 45–53. But the author seems oblivious of the problems raised by his use of the term "labyrinth" to designate what he describes as "the specular temple of Amenhotep" ("specular" because doubled?), contenting himself with evoking in his own analysis the three constituent elements that recur, according to him, in the most diverse contexts: tombs, labyrinths, and rituals (in Egypt, that of the death and resurrection of Osiris).

17. Herodotus, *The History*, 196 (2.148).

18. See Damisch, *Ruptures/Cultures*, 163–64.

19. Marcel Detienne and Jean-Pierre Vernant, *Les Ruses de l'intelligence: La métis des Grecs* (Paris: Flammarion, 1974), 49.

20. Ibid., 41–45.

21. Ibid., 46.

22. Ibid., 47.

23. What follows is greatly indebted to the many brilliant publications, themselves labyrinthine and scattered, at least for the moment, by Pierre Rosenstiehl. Beginning with the text of the lecture he delivered at the same seminar of Roland Barthes on the metaphor of the labyrinth at which I myself dealt with the description of the Egyptian labyrinth. See especially: "Les mots du labyrinthe," in *Cartes et Figures de la terre* (Paris: Centre Georges-Pompidou, 1981), 94–103; "Labyrinthologie mathématique," in *Mathématiques et Sciences humaines* no. 33 (1971): 4–32; "Pour qui ces fils d'Ariane de Beauce et de Toscane," in *La Cifra e l'Immagine*, proceedings of

a conference held in Siena, Italy, July 3–4, 1987; "L'invention du laby-rinthe," in *Le Genre humain* nos. 24–25 (winter–spring 1992): 183–91.

24. Pierre Rosenstiehl, "Les mots du labyrinthe," in *Cartes et Figures de la terre* (Paris: Centre Georges-Pompidou, 1981), 95.

25. Ibid., 97.

26. Pierre Rosenstiehl, "L'invention du labyrinthe," in *Le Genre humain* nos. 24–25 (winter–spring 1992): 186.

27. Ludwig Wittgenstein, *Philosophical Investigations*, trans. G. E. M. Anscombe (New York: The Macmillan Company, 1958), §18, 8.

28. Ibid.

29. On the circle as the most misleading figure of cunning, see M. De-tienne and J.-P. Vernant, *Les ruses de l'intelligence*, 51–52.

30. On the labyrinth as an acentric universe, see Pierre Rosentsiehl, "Les mots du labyrinthe" (as in note 23, above), 102–3. Father Athanasius Kircher seems to have acknowledged the difficulties raised by the ancient descriptions: in the reconstruction of the Egyptian labyrinth in his *Magia Universalis* (Augsbourg: n.p., 1657–1659), the labyrinth is resituated in the center of the complex (see P. Santarcangeli, *Il Libro dei labirinti*, fig. 45).

31. Wittgenstein, *Philosophical Investigations*, §203, 82.

32. Ibid., §534, 144.

33. "Dunraven, who had read a great many detective novels, thought that the solution of a mystery was always a good deal less interesting than the mystery itself; the mystery had a touch of the supernatural and even the divine about it, while the solution was a sleight of hand." Jorge Luis Borges, "Ibn-Hakam al-Bokari, Murdered in His Labyrinth" (from *The Aleph*, 1949), in *Collected Fictions*, trans. Andrew Hurley (New York: Viking Penguin, 1998), 260.

34. Wittgenstein, *Philosophical Investigations*, §123, 49.

35. "A perspicuous representation produces just that understanding which consists in 'seeing connections.' Hence the importance of the discovery and invention of 'intermediate cases.' The concept of a perspicuous representation is of fundamental significance for us. It earmarks the form of account we give, the way we look at things. (Is this a 'Weltanschauung?')" Ibid., §122, 49.

36. "A wish [*wunsch*] seems already to know what will or would not satisfy it; a proposition, a thought, what makes it true—even when that thing is not there at all! Whence this *determining* of what is not yet there? This despotic demand? ('The hardness of the logical must')" (ibid., §437, 129).

"You learned the concept 'pain' when you learned language" (ibid., §384, 118).

CHAPTER 3

1. Roland Barthes, *Empire of Signs*, trans. Richard Howard (New York: Hill & Wang, 1982), 9. On this point as well as on the notion of the line generally, see Hubert Damisch, *Traité du trait* (Paris: Réunion des Musées Nationaux, 1995).

2. Paul Valéry, "Les deux vertus d'un livre," *Oeuvres* (Paris: Gallimard, "Bibliothèque de la Pléiade," 1960), 2:1249. Valéry thought that typography had been brought to its highest level by Didot, on the eve of the Revolution, and by his Italian rival Bodoni of Parma. "Didot the elder designed and realized a typeface that seems to place the texts entrusted to his presses outside of time. One of the final acts of the old monarchy was to engage him, on lavish terms, because of the beauty of his work and the excellence of his art, to print, at state expense, the *Fables* of La Fontaine and other illustrated works" ("Livres," *Oeuvres*, p. 1252).

3. See below, Chap. 6.

CHAPTER 5

1. Jorge Luis Borges, "The Immortal" (from *The Aleph*, 1949), in *Collected Fictions*, trans. Andrew Hurley (New York: Viking Penguin, 1998), 183–95. This citation, 188, emphasis in original.

2. Françoise Choay, *L'Allégorie du patrimoine* (Paris: Éditions du Seuil, 1992).

3. On all of these points (the role of architecture in Hegel's *Aesthetics*; the difference between sign and symbol; and, in general, the values associated with "architecture"), see Denis Hollier, *Against Architecture: The Writings of Georges Bataille*, trans. Betsy Wang (Cambridge, Mass.: MIT Press, c. 1989).

4. Werner Szambien, *Le Musée d'Architecture* (Paris: Picard, 1988).

5. Ibid., 63 and 72.

6. Choay, *L'Allégorie du patrimoine*, 76 ff.

7. Jules Michelet, *Ma jeunesse*, as quoted by Anthony Vidler, "Architecture in the Museum: From Boullée to Lenoir," in *The Writing of the Walls: Architectural Theory in the Late Enlightenment* (Princeton, N.J.: Princeton Architectural Press, 1987), 173.

8. W. Szambien, *Le Musée d'architecture*, 35. See also, by the same author, *Les Projets de l'an II: Concours d'architecture de la période révolutionnaire* (Paris: École Nationale Supérieure des Beaux-Arts, c. 1986).

9. Gabriel-Pierre-Martin Dumont, *Suite de plans . . . des trois temples*

antiques tels qu'ils existaient en 1750 dans le bourg de Paestum et mesurés et dessinés par J.-G. Soufflot (Paris: n.p., 1764).

10. Szambien cites the following passage from Stendhal's *Mémoires d'un touriste* recording his responses to a collection of cork models assembled by an antiquarian in Nîmes—where he had seen it—representing Roman monuments in southern France: "It would be impossible to see imitations that were more skillful and at the same time more accurate. As the [models] are executed to the same scale, for the first time I had an idea of the relative size of these monuments. Monsieur Pelet's pretty buildings have one centimeter for every meter. I saw with astonishment the triumphal arch in Orange, a gigantic structure, pass easily below the lower arches of the Pont du Gard" (Szambien, *Le Musée d'architecture*, 85).

11. Ibid., 34.

12. Vidler, "From the Hut to the Temple: Quatremère de Quincy and the Idea of Type," in *The Writing of the Walls*, 147–64.

13. Szambien, *Le Musée d'architecture*, 15.

14. See Heinz Kaehler, *Hadrian und seine Villa bei Tivoli* (Berlin: n.p., 1950); R. Bianchi-Bandinelli, *Rome: Le centre du pouvoir* (Paris: Gallimard, coll. "L'univers des forms," 1969), 264 ff.

15. Choay, *L'Allégorie du patrimoine*, 28.

16. See Heinz Klotz, "City Wall and Adam's House," in *Museum Architecture in Frankfurt, 1980–1990* (Munich: Prestel, 1990), 150–51.

17. G.-W.-F. Hegel, *Aesthetics: Lectures on Art*, trans. T. M. Knox, 2 vols. (Oxford, Eng.: Clarendon Press, 1975), 2:638–39; see D. Hollier, *Against Architecture*, 13.

18. Jacques Derrida, "Cinquante-deux aphorismes pour un avant-propos" (1986), reprinted in *Psyché* (Paris: Galilée, 1987), 510. I discuss the work of architectural metaphor at length in my preface to a collection of excerpts from Viollet-le-Duc's *Dictionnaire d'architecture française* (*L'Architecture raisonnée* [Paris: Hermann, 1978], 7–29), as well as in "Aujourd'hui, l'architecture" (*Le Temps de la réflexion* II [1981]: 463–80).

19. See *The Renaissance from Brunelleschi to Michelangelo: The Representation of Architecture*, ed. Henry A. Millon and Vittorio Magnago Lampugnani (New York: Rizzoli, 1994). A smaller version of this exhibition was presented in Washington, D.C., and Paris in 1995.

20. See Hubert Damisch, *The Origin of Perspective*, trans. John Goodman (Cambridge, Mass.: MIT Press, 1994).

21. A good example would be the string of small romanesque churches

ringing the city of Tournus, all of which served as experimental structural laboratories for the cathedral.

22. Henry Russell Hitchcock and Philip Johnson, *The International Style* (new ed., New York: W. W. Norton & Company, 1966). First published in 1932.

23. Herbert Bayer, Walter Gropius, and Ise Gropius, *Bauhaus 1919–1928* (Boston: Charles T. Branford, 1959).

24. Philippe Boudon, "L'échelle du schème," in *Images et imaginaires d'architecture*, exhibition catalogue (Paris: Centre Georges-Pompidou, 1984), 49–51.

25. This is confirmed, a posteriori, by the skyscraper designed by Norman Foster for the Commerzbank in Frankfurt, conceived as a "natural tube" (that is, the exact opposite of the Tower of Babel), and which concludes the series begun by Jean Prouvé's design for the National Education Ministry. See Norman Foster & Partners, "Il progetto del grattacielo della Commerzbank a Francoforte," *Casabella* no. 626 (September 1995): 4–17.

CHAPTER 6

1. Georges Duhamel, *Scènes de la vie future* (Paris: Mercure de France, 1930). English translation: *America the Menace: Scenes from the Life of the Future*, trans. Charles Miner Thompson (Boston and New York: Houghton Mifflin Company, 1931).

2. Karl Marx, "Address of the International Workingmen's Association to Abraham Lincoln" (sent to Lincoln on December 30, 1864, and published in the London periodical *Bee-Hive* on January 7, 1865), Karl Marx and Friedrich Engels, *The Civil War in the United States* (New York: International Publishers, 1961), 279–81.

3. Ibid., 282–83.

4. François-René, vicomte de Chateaubriand, *Travels in America*, trans. Richard Switzer (Lexington: University of Kentucky Press, 1969), 193 [translation modified]. First French edition 1828.

5. Marx and Engels, *The Civil War in the United States*, 11.

6. Frederick Jackson Turner, "The Significance of the Frontier in American History" (1894) and "The Problem of the West" (1896), in *Frontier and Section: Selected Essays of Frederick Jackson Turner* (Englewood Cliffs, N.J.: Prentice Hall, 1961), 37–76. See also Richard Hofstadter and Seymour Martin Lipset, eds., *Turner and the Sociology of the Frontier* (New York: Basic Books, 1968).

7. Marx and Engels, *The Civil War in the United States*, 333–34. [This

article, occasioned by the emancipation proclamation and published in *Die Presse* on October 12, 1862, does not appear in English-language editions of this anthology prior to the third, 1961 edition.—Trans.]

8. Chateaubriand, *Travels in America*, 17–20.

9. Alexis de Tocqueville, *Democracy in America*, 2 vols., trans. Henry Reeve, Francis Bowen, and Phillips Bradley (New York: Vintage Books, 1990), 1:14.

10. Ibid., xxi (1848 preface).

11. Ibid., 2:48–52.

12. Stendhal, *The Charterhouse of Parma*, trans. Richard Howard (New York: The Modern Library, 1999), 426.

13. It is a critical commonplace that the architects of Chicago created modern architecture unawares, as though without intending to, by responding to the strictly utilitarian and functional requirements imposed on them by their commissions. As the result of a reversal typical of the American scene, architectural quality has now become a mercantile value there, a speculative and advertising-related consideration, even a criterion of commercial viability figured into a company's financial projections. Architecture should assert itself as such and make itself beautiful (or produce beauty) to sell itself: a state of affairs totally unimaginable (until recently) in France, where only one thing has long been required of architecture, official architecture excepted: that it be nondescript.

14. On this point, see Hubert Damisch, *Théorie du nuage: Pour une histoire de la peinture* (Paris: Éditions du Seuil, 1972), 273–75. English translation forthcoming from Stanford University Press.

15. Michel Eyquem de Montaigne, *The Complete Essays of Montaigne*, trans. Donald M. Frame (Stanford, Calif.: Stanford University Press, 1958), "Of Cannibals," 150–58.

16. Tocqueville, *Democracy in America*, 2:537.

17. Chateaubriand, *Travels in America*, 14–15 [translation modified].

18. Harold Rosenberg, *The Tradition of the New* (New York: Horizon Press, 1961).

19. Jean-Louis Cohen, "L'oncle Sam au pays des Soviets. Le temps des avant-gardes," in J.-L. Cohen and H. Damisch, eds., *Américanisme et Modernité: L'Idéal américain dans l'architecture* (Paris: Flammarion, 1993), 432.

20. Le Corbusier, *When the Cathedrals Were White, a Journey to the Country of Timid People*, trans. Francis E. Hyslop Jr. (New York: Reynal & Hitchcock, [1947]), xxii. First French edition 1937.

21. Blue jeans are a good example. In his *Scritti Corsari* (Milan: Gar-

zanti, 1975), Pasolini denounces the fashion for them on the grounds that they erase all class distinctions, that when someone is wearing them it is difficult to figure out who you're dealing with. The problem becomes more complicated when one considers the high prices young Moscovites were long willing to pay for these articles, which functioned, for them, as symbols of urban America, whereas for the descendants of the pioneers they represented its negation.

22. Morton White and Lucia White, *The Intellectual versus the City: From Thomas Jefferson to Frank Lloyd Wright* (Cambridge, Mass.: MIT Press, 1962).

23. See Harold M. Mayer and Richard C. Wade, *Chicago: Growth of a Metropolis* (Chicago: University of Chicago Press, 1969).

24. Ibid., 103–5.

25. Knut Hamsun, *The Cultural Life of Modern America*, trans. Barbara Gordon Morgridge (Cambridge, Mass.: Harvard University Press, 1969), 29–30.

26. See White and White, *The Intellectual Versus the City*, 128.

27. See Yves Grafmeyer and Isaac Joseph, *L'École de Chicago: Naissance de l'écologie urbaine* (Paris: Auber-Montaigne, 1984).

28. Georg Simmel, in *Soziologie: Untersuchungen über die Formen des Vergesellschaftung* (Leipzig: Duncker & Humblot, 1908); French trans. in Grafmeyer and Joseph, *L'École de Chicago*, 53–60.

29. Paul Morand, *New York* ([New York]: H. Holt and Company, [c. 1930]).

30. See René Thom and Émile Noël, *Prédire n'est pas expliquer: René Thom à la question par Émile Noël* (Paris: Eshel, 1991), 28.

31. Svetlana Alpers, *The Art of Describing: Dutch Art in the Seventeenth Century* (Chicago: University of Chicago Press, 1983), 157.

32. See John A. Kouwenhoven, *The Columbia Historical Portrait of New York: An Essay in Graphic History* (Garden City, N.Y.: Doubleday, 1953).

33. "Perque oculos perit ipse suos" (Ovid, *Metamorphoses*, Book III, v. 440).

34. See Damisch, *The Origin of Perspective*, trans. John Goodman (Cambridge, Mass.: MIT Press, 1994).

35. On this point, see my article on Adolf Loos, "L'autre 'Ich' ou le désir du vide," in Damisch, *Ruptures/Cultures* (Paris: Éditions de Minuit, 1976), 143–59.

36. Thom and Noël, *Prédire n'est pas expliquer*, 49.

CHAPTER 7

1. Le Corbusier, *When the Cathedrals Were White, a Journey to the Country of Timid People*, trans. Frances E. Hyslop Jr. (New York: Reynal & Hitchcock, [1947]), 42. First French edition 1937.

2. Rem Koolhaas, *Delirious New York: A Retroactive Manifesto for Manhattan* (London: Thames & Hudson, 1978).

3. Le Corbusier, *When the Cathedrals Were White*, 90–91.

4. Koolhaas, *Delirious New York*, 10.

5. Ibid., 90.

6. Hugh Ferris, *The Metropolis of Tomorrow* (New York: I. Washburn, 1929).

7. Koolhaas, *Delirious New York*, 100.

8. "A skyscraper should not be a coquettish plume rising straight up from the street. It is a prodigious instrument of concentration, to be placed in the midst of vast open spaces. The density in the skyscraper and the free area at the foot of the skyscraper constitute an indissoluble function. The one without the other is a catastrophe. Just look at New York!" (Le Corbusier, *When the Cathedrals Were White*, 70–71 [translation modified]).

9. It was on the Pont Neuf, while waiting to pick up his glasses from a nearby optician's shop, that Maxime Du Camp conceived the idea of writing about Paris the book that ancient historians had never written about Athens, Rome, or Carthage, a project that Walter Benjamin would take up in turn (see *Charles Baudelaire: A Lyric Poet in the Era of High Capitalism*, trans. Harry Zohn (London: Verso, 1983), Chap. 1, "The Paris of the Second Empire in Baudelaire," 85–86.

10. Walter Gropius, *The New Architecture and the Bauhaus* (London: Faber and Faber, 1935), 30.

11. Kollhaas, *Delirious New York*, 17. On the institution of national parks in America, see below, Chap. 9.

12. Ibid., 170.

13. Freud, *Civilization and its Discontents*, in *SE*, 21 (1961):71.

14. Koolhaas, *Delirious New York*, 111–12.

15. Ibid., 114.

16. Ibid., 7.

17. Erwin Panofsky, "Style and Medium in the Motion-Picture" (1937), reprinted in Daniel Talbot, ed., *Film: An Anthology* (New York: Simon and Schuster, 1959), 15–32.

CHAPTER 8

1. Gilles Deleuze, *Cinema 2: The Time-Image*, trans. Hugh Tomlinson and Robert Galeta (Minneapolis: University of Minnesota, c. 1989), 65.

2. As Alain Masson has noted, this ballet is a parody of the descent into Hell featured in *The Black Crook*, a show produced in 1866 that, according to historians of the musical, initiated the genre (*Comédie musicale* [Paris: Ramsay, 1981], 155–56).

3. Walter Benjamin, "The Work of Art in the Age of Mechanical Reproduction," in *Illuminations*, trans. Harry Zohn (New York: Schocken Books, 1968), 238.

4. Georges Duhamel, *America the Menace: Scenes from the Life of the Future*, trans. Charles Miner Thompson (Boston and New York: Houghton Mifflin Company, 1931), 28.

5. Maurice Merleau-Ponty, *Phenomenology of Perception*, trans. Colin Smith (New York: Humanities Press, 1962), 185 ("The act by which I lend myself to the spectacle must be recognized as irreducible to anything else"). First French edition 1945.

6. Patrick Brion, *La Comédie musicale du "Chanteur de Jazz" à "Cabaret"* (Paris: La Martinière, 1993), 7–8. From the beginning, Broadway paid Hollywood back in its own coin: before departing for the West Coast, Minnelli staged and designed a string of hit shows there featuring satires of Hollywood productions mounted "in black and white." See Vincente Minnelli with Hector Arce, *I Remember It Well* (Garden City, N.Y.: Doubleday & Company, Inc., 1974), 80.

7. In this connection, Minnelli writes of "sliding into the ballet" (ibid.).

8. Morleau-Ponty, *Phenomenology of Perception*, 183–84. Merleau-Ponty was among the first to become interested in the relation between "film and the new psychology." For his article on this subject, see *Sense and Non-Sense*, trans. Hubert L. Dreyfus and Patricia A. Dreyfus (Evanston, Ill.: Northwestern University Press, 1964), 48–59.

9. Minnelli, *I Remember It Well*, 123, 135.

10. "Either the camera will dance or I will. But both of us at the same time—that won't work. A moving camera makes the dancer look as if he's standing still!" Bob Thomas, *Astaire, The Man, the Dancer* (New York: St. Martin's Press, 1984), 213.

11. As Deleuze writes of Fred Astaire and Gene Kelly: "It is like the two extremes of grace as defined by Kleist, 'in the body of a man entirely deprived of consciousness and of the man who possesses an infinite consciousness'" (Deleuze, *Cinema 2: The Time-Image*, 61).

12. On the return of "aura" in the movies, see the special issue of *Art Press,* "Un second siècle pour le cinéma" no. 14 (1994), ed. Dominique Paini, especially the latter's contribution "La trace et l'aura: à propos de *Benny's Video,*" 18–23.

13. Merleau-Ponty, *Phenomenology of Perception,* 180 ("The end of the speech or text will be the lifting of a spell").

14. Deleuze, *Cinema 2: The Time-Image,* 291, n. 25.

15. In *Swingtime* (1936), directed by George Stevens and featuring music by Jerome Kern, Fred Astaire dances a number entitled "Bojangles of Harlem." A further indication of his taste in this matter: at age sixty, he realized his lifelong dream of dancing to the music of Count Basie. Thomas, *Astaire,* 266.

16. Conversely, Bob Thomas notes that orchestra leaders, following Fred Astaire's lead, didn't like Cole Porter's "Night and Day" (one of the great moments in *The Gay Divorcee*) because "the forty-eight bars instead of the usual thirty-two—made it too long" (Thomas, *Astaire,* 75–77).

17. Deleuze, *Cinema 2: The Time-Image,* 62–63.

CHAPTER 9

1. Freud, *Vorlesungen zur Einführung in die Psychoanalyse,* in *GW,* 11:387; *Introductory Lectures on Psycho-Analysis, SE,* 16 (1963):372.

2. Freud, "Formulierungen über die zwei Prinzipen des Psychisches Geschehens," *GW,* 8:234; "Formulations on the Two Principles of Mental Functioning," *SE,* 12 (1958):222, n. 1. On Freud's 1909 trip to the United States, where he had been invited to lecture at Clark University in Worcester, Massachusetts, by its president, Stanley Hall, see Ernest Jones, *The Life and Work of Sigmund Freud,* 3 vols. (New York: Basic Books, 1955), 2:53–59.

3. Freud, "Formulierungen . . . ," *GW,* VIII:235–36; "Formulations . . . ," *SE,* 12:223.

4. See Irmtraud Schaarschmidt-Richter, *Le Jardin japonais* (Fribourg and Paris: Office du Livre, 1979).

5. See above, Chap. 7.

6. See Joseph L. Sax, *Mountains Without Handrails: Reflections on the National Parks* (Ann Arbor: University of Michigan Press, 1980). For a very complete survey of the development of America's national parks, as well as a discussion of the contradictory ideological determinations that shaped them, see also Roderick Nash, *Wilderness and the American Mind* (New Haven, Conn., and London: Yale University Press, 1967).

7. "The concept of aura which was proposed above with reference to historical objects may usefully be illustrated with reference to the aura of

natural ones. We define the aura of the latter as the unique phenomenon of a distance, however close it may be. If, while resting on a summer afternoon, you follow with your eyes a mountain range on the horizon or a branch which casts its shadow over you, you experience the aura of those mountains, of that branch" (Walter Benjamin, "The Work of Art in the Age of Mechanical Reproduction," in *Illuminations*, trans. Harry Zohn (New York: Schocken Books, 1969), 222–23. The French translation by Pierre Klossowski, approved by Benjamin, and the concision of which prompted him to produce a second, rarely quoted version of the essay in German, comes closer—in ways consistent with the dictionary definition of the word—to what is understood in the present book by "skyline": "In short, what is an aura? A singular interweaving of time and space: the unique appearance of something remote, however close it might be. A man who, on a summer afternoon, lets himself follow with his gaze the profile of a mountain range or the line of a branch casting its shadow on him: this man breathes the aura of the mountains, of this branch" ("Qu'est-ce en somme que l'aura? Une singulière trame de temps et d'espace: apparition unique d'un lointain, si proche soit-il. L'homme qui, un après-midi d'été, s'abandonne à suivre du regard le profil d'un horizon de montagnes ou la ligne d'une branche qui jette sur lui son ombre—cet homme respire l'aura de ces montagnes, de cette branche") (Pierre Klossowski, *Écrits français* [Paris: Gallimard, 1991], 144).

8. Alan Trachtenberg, *The Incorporation of America: Culture and Society in the Gilded Age* (New York: Hill and Wang, 1982), 20. On the difference between the discursive spaces specific to landscape painting (and landscape photography) and "scientific" photography, see Rosalind Krauss, "Photography's Discursive Spaces," in *The Originality of the Avant-Garde and Other Modernist Myths* (Cambridge, Mass.: MIT Press, c. 1985), 132–50.

9. See Laura Wood Roper, "The Preliminary Report on the Yosemite and the Big Trees by Frederick Law Olmsted," *Landscape Architecture* XLIII, no. 1 (October 1952): 12–25, cited in J. L. Sax, *Mountains Without Handrails*.

10. See Hans Huth, *Nature and the American: Three Centuries of Changing Attitudes* ([Lincoln]: University of Nebraska Press, 1972), 153.

11. The term "corporation" designates "any association of individuals bound together into a *corpus*, a body sharing a common purpose in a common name" (Trachtenberg, *The Incorporation of America*, 5).

12. See above, Chap. 4.

13. Fred A. Shannon, *The Farmer's Last Frontier 1860–1897* (New York and Toronto: Farrar & Rinehart, Inc. [1945]), cited by Trachtenberg, *The Incorporation of America*, 22.

14. See above, Chap. 6.

15. "What a beautiful and thrilling specimen for America to preserve and hold up to the view of her refined citizens and the world, in future ages! A *nation's park*, containing man and beast, in all the wild and freshness of their nature's beauty!" George Catlin, *Illustrations of the Manners, Customs, and Conditions of the North American Indian*, 2 vols. (London: n.p., 1841), 1:261–62, as cited by Huth, "Yosemite: The Story of an Idea," *Sierra Club Bulletin*, 1948. New edition Yosemite Natural Association, 1984, where this passage appears on page 8. The very title of this text—which first appeared as a letter addressed by Catlin to the *New York Daily Commercial Advisor*, for which he covered the Indian territories—implies an entire program.

16. Commenting on this word, J. L. Sax (*Mountains Without Handrails*, 47) goes so far as to associate certain recreations with specific professional and/or social classes: fly casting with businessmen, snowmobiling with blue-collar workers, and so forth.

17. Sigmund Freud, *The Complete Letters of Sigmund Freud to Wilhelm Fliess, 1887–1904*, trans. and ed. by Jeffrey Moussaieff Masson (Cambridge, Mass., and London: The Belknap Press of Harvard University Press, 1985). See Jean Laplanche and Jean-Bertrand Pontalis, *The Language of Psycho-Analysis*, trans. Donald Nicholson-Smith (New York and London: W. W. Norton & Company, 1973), "Topography; Topographical," 449–53.

18. Oliver Wendell Holmes, "Phi Beta Kappa Address" (1870), and George M. Beard, *American Nervousness* (1884), cited by Trachtenberg, *The Incorporation of America*, 45, 47–48.

19. Laplanche and Pontalis, *The Language of Psycho-Analysis*), "Ego-Ideal," 184–86.

20. Freud, "Formulierungen . . . ," *GW*, 8:236–37; "Formulations . . . ," *SE*, 12:224.

21. Trachtenberg, *The Incorporation of America*, 7–8.

22. See the classic text by Ernst Kantorowicz, *The King's Two Bodies: A Study in Medieval Political Theology* (Princeton, N.J.: Princeton University Press, 1957).

23. "The Significance of the Frontier," in *Frontier and Section: Selected Essays of Frederick Jackson Turner* (Englewood Cliffs, N.J.: Prentice Hall, 1961), 39. See Trachtenberg, *The Incorporation of America*, 16.

24. Trachtenberg, *The Incorporation of America*, 59–60.

25. William C. Bryant, preface to *Picturesque America* (1874), cited in ibid., 18–19. So enormous are the great California sequoias that in 1853, when a group of eager entrepreneurs stripped a few particularly gigantic

trees of their bark and shipped it to Europe for exhibition at fairs there, the project miscarried, for no one believed that trees of such size could possibly exist (J. L. Sax, *Mountains Without Handrails*, 7). On the relation of the Trojan War to the beginning of European history, see Hubert Damisch, *The Judgment of Paris*, trans. John Goodman (Chicago and London: University of Chicago Press, 1996).

26. P. Reyner Banham, *Scenes in America Deserta* (Cambridge, Mass.: Harvard University Press, 1989), 86. First published 1982.

27. "In the path of America's future seemed to lie a *natural* history that gave to the Western settlement a biblical cast" (Trachtenberg, *The Incorporation of America*, 18).

28. Friedrich Nietzsche, *Thus Spake Zarathustra*, Part IV, *The Portable Nietzsche*, ed. and trans. Walter Kaufmann (New York: Viking Press, 1954), 417.

29. Martin Heidegger, *What Is Called Thinking?*, trans. J. Glenn Gray (New York: Harper & Row, [1968]), 30. "We have invented happiness— say the last men, and they blink" (F. Nietzsche, *Also Sprach Zarathustra*). On the meaning of the "blink" to which modern man is reduced here, and which characterizes his inability "to subject himself to himself, and to despise what is despicable in his kind as it is so far," see Heidegger, ibid., 59–63.

30. Hannah Arendt, *The Human Condition* (Chicago and London: University of Chicago Press, 1958), 231–32.

31. Heidegger, *What Is Called Thinking?*, 49.

32. Ibid.

33. Hannah Arendt, *Qu'est-ce que la politique*, ed. Ursula Ludz; trans. [from *Was Ist Politik?*] Sylvie Courtine-Denamy (Paris: Seuil, 1995), 136–39, frag. 4 "*Du désert et des oasis (un chapitre de conclusion possible)*."

34. Hannah Arendt and Karl Jaspers, *Hannah Arendt Karl Jaspers Correspondence 1926–1969*, ed. Lotte Kohler and Hans Saner; trans. Robert and Rita Kimber (New York and London: Harcourt Brace Jovanovich, c. 1992), letter of February 6, 1955, 251.

35. Nietzsche, *Thus Spake Zarathustra*, Part IV, in *The Portable Nietzsche*, 421.

36. Heidegger, *What Is Called Thinking*, 60: "For he who passes over must pass away; the superman's way begins with his passing away."

37. "'The march, the desert' ('Bad Blood') are indissociable. Which preceded the other? Marching onward enlarges the desert: 'this can only be the end of the world, being pushed forward' ('Childhood')" (Alain

Borer, *Rimbaud, l'heure de la fuite* [Paris: Gallimard, coll. "Découvertes," 1991], 92).

38. Jorge Luis Borges, "The Two Kings and the Two Labyrinths" (from *The Aleph*, 1949), in *Collected Fictions*, trans. Andrew Hurley (New York: Viking Penguin, 1998), 264.